Envisioning
a Lutheran Communion
Perspectives for the Twenty-First Century

Mark Thomsen
Vítor Westhelle
Editors

Kirk House Publishers
Minneapolis, Minnesota

Envisioning a Lutheran Communion
Perspectives for the Twenty-first Century

Mark Thomsen & Vítor Westhelle, Editors

Acknowledgements

The Lutheran School of Theology at Chicago acknowledges a grant from the Division for Global Mission of he Evangelical Lutheran Church in America which made publication of this volume possible.

The vision for a 50 year celebration of the Lutheran World Federation anniversary focused on the future and prophetic voices from the third world. The chapters in this book are the presentations at that celebration at the Lutheran School of Theology at Chicago.

Library of Congress Cataloging-in Publication Data
Envisioning a Lutheran communion / Mark Thomsen, Vítor Westhelle, editors
     p.cm.
  Includes bibliographic references
  ISBN 1-886513-29-5 (alk. paper)
    1. Lutheran World Federation—Congresses. I. Thomsen, Mark W.,
    1931- II. Westhelle, Vítor, 1952-
BX8004.L9 E58 2002
284.1--dc21

2002028518

Kirk House Publishers, PO Box 390759, Minneapolis, MN 55439
Manufactured in the United States of America

Preface

The publication of this book is an important contribution to the ongoing process which is expressed in the book's title, "Envisioning a Lutheran Communion." This book gathers the reports of a distinguished international group of Lutherans, presented at a colloquium convened by the Lutheran School of Theology at Chicago (LSTC), October 1-5, 1998. Furthermore, it was an occasion for the LWF member churches in North America to celebrate the fiftieth anniversary of the Lutheran World Federation. It builds on the major work published on the occasion of the LWF fiftieth anniversary in 1997, "From Federation to Communion: The History of the Lutheran World Federation." In the present book, we encounter a rich tapestry of contexts and challenges, which together represent the rainbow of God's gifts within the Lutheran communion of churches. All of this reminds us of the cries of God's people, and the whole of creation, for hope and healing.

I am indeed grateful to the Lutheran School of Theology at Chicago for their vision and generosity in hosting the colloquium and in publishing this collection of papers. It reflects their longstanding commitment to the intimate and practical aspects of theological and missiological study and global relationships of the church. The very act of bringing together such an international colloquium brings life to the vision of a Lutheran communion. In an important sense, the purpose of the LWF is made clear when such a diversity of prophetic voices speaks as one voice with a challenge and call focused on the vision of communion. The inclusion of such diverse contexts and cultures aptly expresses the oikumene to which we all belong.

In celebrating the milestone of the LWF's fiftieth anniversary, the theme of the colloquium, "Prophetic Voices: Envisioning a Lutheran Communion—Perspectives for the Twenty-first Century," looks to the flow of history and human relations which puts before us the challenge of tomorrow. In this sense, "prophetic voices" must speak from the integrity of our origins and commitments; "envisioning a Lutheran communion" invites creative expressions of a common future; and "perspectives for the twenty-first century" grounds us in the practical reality of life which is lived at the start of a new century, indeed, of a new millennium.

The launching of the LWF in 1947, with its vision for a global Lutheran movement, was a bold step, given the political context of those times. It was a complex exercise that brought people and communities together who, although sharing essentially the same confession and theological heritage, had obvious cultural and political differences. It was a prophetic act, rooted in faith and hope, which set the tone for a Lutheran communion whose mission is to provide visible expressions of Christian unity, justice, peace and reconciliation in the face of seemingly insurmountable forces of division.

In this context of "who we claim to be as a communion," the writers represented here are the prophetic voices who issue the challenges and call for faithful response. Among the voices, Rev. Mitri Raheb, from Palestine, envisions the church transforming "the enemy into a neighbor" as a sign of this communion. Rev. Wanda Deifelt, from Brazil, emphasizes that to understand one another, one must "assume a partiality on behalf of the other." Rev. Molefe Tsele, from South Africa, observes that modern Lutheranism has become "quietistic and conservative" as he highlights growing economic disparities that result in groups of "have-alls and have-nothings." Dr. Monica Melanchthon, from India, affirms that "women seek a kinder, gentler, less rigidly 'gendered' world," emphasizing that "assimilation with the dominant is not good enough." In historical perspective, Rev. Vitor Westhelle, from Brazil and the USA, concludes that, through its history, the overall trend of the Lutheran World Federation has been "toward the recognition of the voice of the other."

The publication of this collection of papers comes a few years after the colloquium, at a time when the member churches of the LWF are preparing to gather for the LWF Tenth Assembly, 21-31 July 2003, in Winnipeg, Canada. The theme of the Tenth Assembly, "For the Healing of the World," could easily have been the focus of one of the papers at the colloquium at LSTC in 1998. Throughout the world, the divisions, conflicts and injustices are, in some ways, deeper today than those wounding the globe in 1947, the year of the LWF's founding. Today's harsh realities yearn for the expression of hope which is embodied in the Assembly theme.

Therefore, it is fitting that the Lutheran School of Theology at Chicago has chosen to dedicate this book to the LWF Tenth Assembly. It brings the celebration and vision of the colloquium, "Envisioning a Lutheran Communion," into the setting of the Assembly and its theme. More particularly, it invites a global audience of readers and the participants who will gather at the Assembly in Winnipeg, to continue the process of engaging God's vision for the healing of the world.

Ishmael Noko

General Secretary

Lutheran World Federation

Foreword: A Biblical Reflection

Barbara Rossing

How do we recognize a prophet in our generation? What are the identifying criteria for God's prophetic voices in the world today?

In biblical times prophets could be recognized by the prophetic mantle, a particular cloak that symbolized the mantle of God's spirit. Before being taken up in the whirlwind the prophet Elijah cast his mantle over Elisha, symbolizing the handing on of the prophetic vocation to the next generation.

Elijah's prophetic mantle must have been distinctive in appearance. When fifty prophets saw Elisha on the road wearing this cloak, even from far away they recognized from the mantle that "the spirit of Elijah has settled on Elisha" (2 Kings 2:15).

So what does the prophetic mantle look like in our communion? What is its distinctive appearance today? The Lutheran World Federation is fifty years old. We give thanks for our predecessors, for their prophetic voices. And now we ask: who are the next generation of prophetic voices? Who wears Elijah's mantle now? On whom is God's spirit settling?

Or perhaps prophecy has ceased in our time. The ancient Jewish historian Flavius Josephus argued that because the orderly succession of prophets had been broken, prophecy had ended in Israel.[1] But Christians must disagree with Josephus' pronouncement. The mantle of God's spirit continues to fall on many shoulders, raising up prophets in many places: in Nazareth, in Bethlehem, in Johannesburg, South Africa; in Gurukul, India; in Sao Leopoldo, Brazil; in Geneva, Switzerland; even in Chicago. Prophecy does not always follow the orderly succession that Josephus mandated. Indeed, the church is in danger when we try to impose criteria of orderly succession on God's spirit.

Luke 7 is a New Testament chapter about prophetic succession, depicting people's attempts to determine whether or not Jesus was a prophet. Like Elijah, Jesus had raised a widow's son from the dead; like Elisha, he had healed people and fed them; he had preached the word of God. Had the mantle of prophet now fallen on Jesus' shoulders? Witnessing Jesus' deeds, the crowd makes this connection back to the prophetic tradition of Elijah and Elisha, acclaiming that "A great prophet has arisen among us!"

But other people were more skeptical about Jesus. At dinner, Jesus' allowing of a sinful woman from anointing and touching him suggests to Simon, the host, that Jesus "must not be a prophet, or surely he would know what kind of woman is touching him" (Luke 7:39). True prophets would know such things about the people who touch them, after all.

Even John the Baptist cannot tell whether or not Jesus is a prophet. Stuck in prison, John sends out his emissaries to try to find out the answer. But Jesus won't tell them Yes or No. Instead, Jesus answers John with a set of criteria: "the blind receive their sight, the lame walk, the deaf hear, the dead are raised, the poor have good news preached to them; and blessed is anyone who takes no offense at me." These are Jesus' criteria for authentic prophetic ministry.

This conference brings together some current prophetic voices whom God is raising up in the Lutheran communion worldwide. We welcome these messengers' prophetic words. We welcome their vision and counsel for how the church can be a prophetic voice in the world.

Look more closely at Jesus' list of criteria in Luke 7, to see what God's spirit might be saying to us at this moment in history. If Jesus' words in Luke 7 set criteria for prophets, then we must attend to such things as healing--- how the blind can receive sight and the deaf hear. The Lutheran World Federation's 2003 theme, "for the healing of the world," emphasizes the healing dimension of our prophetic ministry.

If Luke 7 sets prophetic criteria then we must attend also to economic issues--- how the poor can experience good news in the midst of economic globalization and economic crises. What is the spirit of God saying to churches at this moment in our history when the gap between rich and poor is widening?

If Jesus' care for the marginalized people in Luke 7 is a criterion for authentic prophecy—his action of raising of a widow's child, his welcome of the woman who was a sin- ner—then we too must listen to the marginalized today, to women, children, gay and lesbian people and others whom the church tends to marginalize. Bishop Leontyne Kelly, the first African American bishop in the United Methodist church, tells how at her christening as a tiny baby the bishop said of her "How I wish you were a boy so that my mantle could fall on you." Too often, the church continues to deny recognition when the prophetic mantle when it falls on girls or women or others who do not meet its criteria. The presenters at this conference share provocative insights on these prophetic issues.

Who are other prophetic voices in the Lutheran commun- ion? Who else wears Elijah's mantle today, the mantle of God's spirit? Look again at Luke 7, Jesus' enigmatic tribute to John the Baptist in the ranks of God's realm. John is very great, yes, Jesus says. Yet "the least in the kingdom of God is greater" than John. This is one of the most amazing state- ments in this passage.

Look further: "Wisdom is vindicated by all of her chil- dren," Jesus says (Luke 7:35)—that is, by all of us. God's Wisdom is vindicated not just by a few lone prophets but by all of God's people in our prophetic calling.

So take up that prophetic mantle. Wear Elijah's cloak like an invisible mantle around your shoulders. Say Yes to the voice of God's prophetic spirit in the world. Say yes to the many prophetic voices God is raising up in our generation and in our successors—in our children, in the marginalized, in voices from around the world, and in the next generation.

An Invitation for a Global Table-Talk

William Lesher

It is a unique privilege for me to return to The Lutheran School of Theology at Chicago (LSTC) and to say a word at the outset of this historic event. It is especially a privilege to have the opportunity to address people who are being, or who have been, formed academically in this place, a place that over the years has been very intentional in building an international ecumenical doctoral program under the leadership of a distinguished Lutheran faculty. I had not thought of it quite this way before but here gathered to celebrate the 50th anniversary of the Lutheran World Federation, I think we could cautiously and gratefully make the observation—just among ourselves—that LSTC has been the main expression of the LWF in the field of graduate studies in the USA. So it makes a lot of sense that this 50th anniversary celebration should be held here; that the speakers at the event are mostly people who are graduates of this place and its doctoral program; and that those of us gathered here should take a few moments to think about the importance of this event.

Allow me then to make a few points about the importance of what is happening here in the next few days and your role in it.

T.S. Elliot wrote:

We shall not cease from exploration;

and the end of all our exploring

Will be to arrive at where we started;

and know the place for the first time.

Every gathering of the LWF is, in one sense, an exploration of the Word of God as that Word is understood in the Evangelical Reformation Tradition and as that tradition is filtered through the experiences of people from an increasing number of different cultures and personal histories. When we come together from our various countries and cultures, it is never exactly the same as it was the last time. There are always some new conditions in our global context, and most often there are some new voices and some new regions represented. When we read the familiar texts and sing the hymns, some worn and tested, some fresh and yet to be tested, and when we make our common confession, it is to know this faith, this Christ, and this communion in a new and ever-changing way. That is to say, this celebration with you here and with many younger scholars from this doctoral program from around the world as speakers and leaders will be like none other-- not like Hong Kong, not like Geneva, not like the many other places where this milestone is marked. Why? Because those who gather here will bring to this event precisely that which Jesus says characterizes the Kingdom (Matthew 13:52): they will bring out of the treasure-house of the past, something old and out of their experiences in many different places and out of their visions of the future from many different perspective something entirely new, and by the end of the event, quite possibly, with God's grace and with the Spirit's leading, we will know this fellowship, this organization, this global communion, as if for the first time.

Second, we stand at the threshold of an opportune and ominous moment -- the two contradictory or complimentary sides of every propitious time in history. God in God's grace has brought us to life and to ministry at a time when this particular faith family -- 65 million in 60 nations around the world -- is more conscious of itself and more connected to its many parts through the miracle of modern communication than ever before. In a period of global fragmentation we, together with people of other faith communities, can be a unique kind of "global glue."

This new awareness and this new self-conscious began to dawn at the start of this decade as delegates to the Eighth Assembly in Curitiba redefined the LWF as a world-wide "communion" of people who hold far more than an organization in common. Baptism, as our primary ordination, a Gospel centered in unmerited grace, and a common global mission of justification and justice -- these are much more the marks of our global bond. At Hong Kong, the Ninth Assembly of the LWF, said yes again to the notion of a global Lutheran sense of communion and prescribed to employ fully the new communication technologies in the service of our growing global sense of ourselves.

Technology makes it possible for us to be present to each other as never before. But the question is, "How will we use these new gifts?" From a North American perspective it is clear that without the input and critique from colleagues around the world, we cannot do theology adequately or responsibly in our highly globalized context. There is a chance that in applying the new technology, we can bear one another's burden in new ways. We can be in communication with one another, seminary-to-seminary, church-to-church, congregation-to-congregation and even person-to-person, in ways we have not yet imagined. Think how our pastoral practices can be enriched as we learn from one another and as we begin to envision the world as a parish and ourselves ministering in our place on behalf of the whole global Lutheran parish. Images shape our thoughts and our behavior. The image, of a global Lutheran Communion in communication with itself is an image to shape our future.

Finally, we celebrate what has been and we project ourselves into that which is not yet, precisely at a time when the religions of the world are being challenged to be a force for global reconciliation. Hans Kung's prophetic utterance at the Parliament of the World's Religions in Chicago (1993) indicates what must be a major part of our mission in the new millennium: "There will be no peace on earth until there is peace among the religions of the world."

We Lutherans are, of course, even in our "bigness" a very small clan within the global Christian family. Through the Lutheran World Federation our reconciling efforts with Rome, with the Alliance of Reformed Churches, and with Lambeth are urgent, simply signaling to the world that Christ is over all of our cultures. Though we are nourished and though we minister out of very concrete and different contexts, it is important to demonstrate that our final loyalty is to a Cosmic Christ who is the Alpha and Omega, not of Lutherans, not even of Christians but of all humanity and of the whole creation.

As the LWF declared in its theme back in Minneapolis in 1957 "Christ Frees and Unites." One of our greatest opportunities (with ominous consequences if we fail) is to learn how the freedom we have in Christ can lead us to a greater unity with all of God's people; with those of the Christian faith and with those of the other great faith families of the world.

Well, soon the celebration will begin. The stadium will be filled. The Church will gather. But before the celebration begins, let us remember the blessing of our calling that brings us to this place and to this task, and let us pray that the words spoken here and the meditations and reflections of all the hearts and heads gathered here will do honor to all that has been and point a faithful and obedient way to that which is not yet.

The Future of the Lutheran Communion

Ishmael Noko

For a very long time prior to 1947, Lutherans in Europe and North America had wanted to foster a global Lutheran organization for Lutheran cooperation and for the sake of Christian unity and witness. The early initiatives were interrupted by the two devastating "European" World Wars. Then, fifty years ago last year, North American Lutherans were scheduled to host the first Assembly of the Lutheran World Federation. However, for a variety of reasons, the venue was changed from Philadelphia, USA, to Lund, Sweden.

In considering the future of the present Lutheran communion, we would do well to take into consideration its history and basic purpose. In this regard, the recently published book on the LWF entitled *From Federation to Communion: History of the Lutheran World Federation* is a salutary resource for readers interested. Published in 1997 as a contribution to the celebration of the LWF's 50th anniversary, the book provides a wealth of information about the Federation's past, which is crucially relevant to its future. In reading this quite accessible book, one comes to the conclusion that the launching of the LWF in 1947 with its vision for a global Lutheran movement was "more that a human act," especially when one recalls that the founding delegates themselves came from nations which only a few months prior to Lund had been at war with each other. It was a prophetic response to the *kairos* of God, and as such, this early prophetic act, rooted in faith and hope, set the tone for a

Lutheran communion, whose mission was to provide visible expressions of Christian unity, justice, peace, and reconciliation in the face of seemingly insurmountable forces of division.

As most of you will recall, in July 1997 the Lutheran World Federation held its Ninth Assembly in the cosmopolitan city of Hong Kong, seven days after that island-city was returned to China. The 50th anniversary of the LWF was celebrated by delegates, church representatives, the staff of the Federation, and ecumenical guests. It was a times of reflection, repentance and thanksgiving. We observed that since the formation of the LWF, much has changed both in the Federation and in the world. We observed that the LWF has not only increased its membership numerically, but has also increased the quality of the fellowship and deepened it to the extent that the term *Federation* no longer adequately describes the nature of that fellowship. We observed that in the process of the churches growing together the earlier "Euro-America" numerical dominance of the LWF has been demographically transformed, so to speak, into a "rainbow" communion where people of different regions - women, men, young and old - all have space in its life and work.

On the same occasion we noted with regret that half a century after the founding of the Federation, as we stand at the threshold of a new century and millennium, we live in an interdependent world and yet we are riven by divisions as deep, if not deeper, that those wounding the globe in 1947. These divisions are expressed on different levels and in different ways in our nations and societies. Allow me to elaborate on some of these divisions.

Abuse of power. Power relationships between our nations and within our societies continue to be conducted in a competitive, confrontational, and divisive manner. The possession of power calls for responsible stewardship in the use of that power, which includes the responsibility to use that power with sensitivity and with justice. By dealing with each other sensitively and justly we could avoid the negative consequences which so often follow the arrogant or insensitive application of power by dominant nations, societies,, and individuals. Division, conflict, and exclusion of the "other" seem even to be woven into the fabric of democracy, with partisan politics becoming increasingly vicious and implacable.

Inequity. A true partnership between women and men in church and society is still an unrealized goal. In many societies, women still struggle for the rights and the opportunities which men take for granted. The history of the church demonstrates beyond a doubt how we have failed continuously to adhere to St. Paul's injunction that in Christ "there is neither Jew, nor Greek, male nor female." Is it not unfortunate that for ages the mainline churches have tried to proclaim the gospel by placing the primary responsibility on one gender? Most of us, I want to believe, now know that such a division is no longer sustainable. The gospel was never intended to be proclaimed by one gender alone. Such a situation, never justifiable, it is theologically incompatible with our understanding of the whole church as a priesthood of all believers. A genuine and just partnership of women and men called in Christ to proclaim the word of promise to the world *is a way forward* for the church and consequently for the Lutheran communion.

Ecumenicity. In the ecumenical sphere, there have been very encouraging signs of engagement and cooperation at different levels. The decades of ecumenical dialogues at international and regional levels have produced a rich harvest which we are now reaping. The Joint Declaration with the Roman Catholic Church and the regional conversations with the Reformed and Episcopal churches are fine fruits, indeed. However, we must also recognize that there are to this day many, many theological and non-theological issues that remain resistant to the tide of dialogue. Therefore, the shadow of disunity still dogs us, and the cherished goal of "visible unity" remains elusive.

Church conflict. Within individual churches, we also continue, sadly, to encounter situations of conflict, of division, and of distrust. They challenge our expressed commitments to reconciliation and unity. In addition, our theological language persistently fails to communicate effectively the relevance of our reflections upon the nature of God's grace to laity in congregations. We present our thoughts and message in theological formulations that only a few can decipher. Thus we indirectly deny the majority of our church members the professional theological assistance to which they are entitled. We must find ways to "democratize" and disseminate our theological reflections, as the lifeblood of a living church.

Economic divisions. Economic divisions cut deeply through this "globalized" world. The widening disparities between rich and poor nations — the North and the South — are increasingly apparent. They are actively being thrown into even sharper and more tragic relief by the current global financial crisis.

Within nations, even wealthy nations, the same widening gaps between rich and poor can be observed. The recently released United Nations Report on Human Development indicates that the United States, although the largest and strongest economy in the world, has groups of people that include the poorest of the industrialized countries when measured in broader human development terms.

Contrary to the rhetoric, the processes of international economic liberalization have not produced increased prosperity for all. I believe that we now have enough experience with international economic policies and their effects upon people at the grassroots to say that the opposite is the case. Rich nations and rich individuals have enjoyed the advantages of increased prosperity from selective economic globalization and have been insulated better from shocking economic fluctuation, while the poor have paid the price. This model of economic life does not show signs of promoting human dignity, but rather fosters sharp divisions based upon self-interest.

Fundamentalism. A rising tide of fundamentalism of all kinds acts as a serious obstacle to mutual understanding, respect for one another, and peace among nations. Religious fundamentalism is a never-ending challenge to our most cherished ideals of religious freedom for all. It destroys those channels of communication that are prerequisite to effective dialogue and cooperation between different faith-based communities.

Ethnic conflicts. Ethnic conflicts and tensions seem more bitter and violent than ever. The human catastrophes in the Great Lakes region of Africa, in Bosnia, and in Kosovo still wound our memories. The conflicts in the Middle East continue more than ever to demand an effective response from the international community. Racial discrimination also divides our societies, as reflected in the burning of church buildings in black communities of this country. Indigenous peoples have been excluded from and disenfranchised by our societies. They call for land rights and respect for their traditional cultures and laws.

Lutheran response. The question before us is this: How will the Lutheran communion respond to these realities and trends? The answer brings us back to the original purpose for which the Federation was founded in 1947: to *foster a global Lutheran cooperation for the sake of Christian unity and witness*, despite the forces and obstacles which divide us. The past of the LWF is also its future. The common faith and the sense of hope which inspired the formation of the LWF must be the beacon to guide this communion as we confront divisions, conflicts, and injustices that beset us and the world on the verge of a new century and a new millennium. Only in that faith and in that hope will we have the strength to transcend the obstacles which seem to block the path to reconciliation, unity, and justice.

Christ-centeredness. In faith and hope, we can envision a Jerusalem which is not a city of divisions and conflict, but a city of peace, both spiritually and politically. As we enter the third millennium, it is essential that we remind ourselves again and again the celebration of the millennium was the 2000th anniversary celebration of the birth of Christ. It afforded us an opportune time to reflect on both the spiritual and political significance of the city of Jerusalem. We can imagine again a city of two peoples, a city holy to three faiths, a city at peace with itself, and a model for peace and reconciliation in the world. And we can work and pray together for it to happen.

Debt forgiveness. In faith and hope, we can envision a world in which obviously unrepayable debt is not allowed to remain like a millstone around the necks of poor nations. Such debts prevent a generation of children from enjoying basic health care, safe water, and education. Rather, we can imagine a world where, in global solidarity and compassion, unrepayable debt is canceled in the spirit of Jubilee for the sake of the children. We cannot quibble about credit-worthiness and structural adjustments. Debt relief should embrace the individual, lift the burden from the shoulders of those who bear its heaviest weight, and remember the unborn child. And we can work and pray together for it to happen.

Human rights. In faith and hope, we can envision a world in which nations agree that it is not wise to protect national sovereignty which allows the perpetrators of massive violations of human rights and international humanitarian law to escape prosecution. Rather, we can imagine a global consensus on an effective and independent mechanism that brings those who have committed such crimes to justice, regardless of their national or political affiliations. The victims of such crimes deserve justice and access to compensation and rehabilitation. Some effective deterrent must be found to protect others who might become the victims of such crimes in the future. An international criminal court, as proposed and sketched out in Rome earlier this year, would have the potential to contribute to these goals. And we can work and pray together for it to become a reality.

Landmines outlawed. In faith and hope, we can envision a world in which anti-personnel landmines are not sown in the earth to bring forth a harvest of maimed bodies and crippled communities. Rather, we can imagine the complete abolition of the manufacture, stockpiling, and use of these cruel and indiscriminate weapons. No more innocent children, no more women fetching water, no more struggling communities need to feel their pitiless effects. And we can work and pray together for it to happen.

Intergovernmental forums. In faith and hope, we can envision a world in which military and/or economic dominance are not the criteria for resolving disputes between nations. Rather, we can imagine effective, respected, and properly resourced intergovernmental forums in which dialogue, the rule of law and ethics will resolve issues of contention. And we can work and pray together for these things to happen.

Interfaith agreements. In faith and hope, we can envision a world in which members of different faiths find in their respective faiths no inherent cause for conflict or tension. Rather, we can imagine a continuous and open dialogue with people of their faiths in which we can celebrate our agreements and explore without animosity our differences, finding ways in which we can cooperate and work together. And we can work and pray together for these things to happen.

Theological renewal. In faith and hope, we can envision our theological schools and other church institutions not as places of disputation and conflict, but as nurseries and as testing grounds for ideas for theological renewal to enrich and inform the lives of our churches. We can begin to see the larger role of these schools and institutions not only in supporting the vision and ministries of our local and national churches, but as providers of theological education for the wider Lutheran family and the ecumenical movement. We can envision a Lutheran communion of churches which reflects in its life and practice the unity to which we are called, participating fully in the "unity in diversity" of the wider ecumenical family. And we can work and pray together for it to happen.

Church unity. In faith and hope, we can envision a Lutheran communion that holds up high the reminder that for the Confessio Augustana of 1530, which was drafted by Martin Luther's party, was intended for the entire church. In this regard, ecumenism is not one of the many activities on a list of options from which the LWF may choose, but is an integral part of what it means to be Lutheran. In pursuing this imperative we recognize fully that the true unity of the church, which is its unity as the body of Christ, is given in and through the proclamation of the Gospel in Word and in Sacrament. This unity is expressed as communion in the common and at the same time multiform confession of the one and same apostolic faith.

The LWF is a partial expression of the wider *koinonia*, the body of Christ. It cannot exist in isolation from the wider expression of the church catholic. Through bilateral ecumenical dialogues and relationships, the Lutheran communion is making a genuine contribution toward the search for Christian unity. In recent decades we have had dialogues with other Christian World Communions (CWC) which resulted in growing doctrinal convergences. In some instances, we have overcome old antagonisms and rescinded some doctrinal condemnations.

In faith and hope, we envision an ecumenical century in which the ecumenical harvest will encompass the rich piety and the theological and spiritual insights of those communities who are so often forgotten, such as Diaspora, minority and refugees who are silenced or made invisible by forces of dominance in our churches and society.

In faith and hope, I personally envision a Lutheran communion whose faith is rooted in the apostolic tradition; a communion willing to take courageous steps forward in search of a New World Order in which the concept of fundamental human dignity and human rights of all people will provide for a just and peaceful future.

The Church as witness. It is quite clear that the founders of the LWF in 1947 and in subsequent years shared in the Biblical view that every human being is created in the image of God. They also shared the conviction that through the cross of Calvary, God was in Christ not only suffering, but publicly declaring that human life is life in freedom—a gift from God. The church as the body of Christ is called to be a bold and living witness to God's good news for the world. To shrink away from this responsibility undermines the credibility of the witness. The church as the body of Christ lives and shares in the pain and suffering of the witness. The church as the body of Christ lives and shares in the pain and suffering of the community and in doing so bears witness to God's love and compassion.

This, I think, constitutes part of our future. Any lesser goal would fail to live up to the vision, faith,` and hope of those who, against the tide of history, put aside their differences and joined together to form what today is the Lutheran communion.

50 Years of LWF Mission and Service

By Dorothy J. Marple

Celebrating 50 years of LWF history seems natural. After all, we recognize 50th wedding anniversaries, 50th high school and college reunions, 50 years as an ordained pastor—and then there's the big 50th birthday!

In terms of human history fifty years is hardly a tick in time. Yet these past 50 years have been extremely significant to Lutherans worldwide - in coming together as a communion of churches, in finding common pathways for witness and service, and in seeking justice and peace. We honor the efforts of many people all around the world, some well-known and some not so well-known, people who have helped shape, undergird, advance, even agitate and stir the Federation to move forward. A look at the past 50 years, even a very brief look, shows that the bits and pieces of decisions and events, of speeches and reports, of meetings and minutes, begin to form continuous threads in fulfilling the purposes of the Federation.

This is a brief history of the Lutheran World Federation emphasizing the major achievements, gifts, and traditions, which the LWF brings to the contemporary Lutheran communion. This will obviously not be "LWF History 101" or even an historical survey in forty minutes. The editors of *From Federation to Communion: The History of the Lutheran World Federation*[1] present the LWF story as an historical survey, and that work took 552 pages! I will focus on some key events of service and mission which reflect the vision of the LWF at its founding. Your list of highlights may be different as you reflect on the LWF from your experience. We all have participated in the LWF history in one way or another.

As Gottfried Brakemeier, past president of the Federation, said at the Hong Kong Assembly, "The Lutheran World Federation has no permanent home on this earth. . . it is present wherever its member churches are located."[2] Thus the LWF story certainly is not only that of the Secretariat in Geneva. The relationships among the member churches, large and small, dominant and minority, older and emerging, and the overarching patterns of cooperation within the Federation are all integral to the LWF story.

The LWF today is not what it was 50 years ago. It is different! Picture, for example, the First Assembly in 1947 with about 200 delegates, nearly all of them men, many in clerical garb, processing down a quiet street in the quiet town of Lund, Sweden, to a stately twelfth-century cathedral for the opening worship. Then recall fifty years later, the stainless steel and glass convention center in Hong Kong, flanked by river traffic in the harbor on the one side and by the busyness and noise of a modern city on the other. Those 385 delegates, some of them in national dress and about half of them women, hurry along polished floors and use escalators to reach the auditorium for opening ceremonies.

From the beginning there has been something in the very being of the LWF that has enabled the Federation to seek unity and to cohere and endure at times despite severe testing as controversies and debates over theological and policy matters arose and hard decisions were made. That something went beyond reaching consensus or a majority vote to a more profound recognition of the deep bonds of unity made possible through the life of Christ and working of the Holy Spirit.

This deeper meaning of unity has been in part the wellspring for the Federation's becoming more inclusive. The inclusion of the Lutheran churches of the South, of women, of youth, and of persons with disabling conditions has enlarged the capacity of the Federation to make a united witness to

Christ. The summons to full inclusiveness has been sounded clearly even as the deeper meanings of unity and the concern for justice and human rights are still to be realized.

Assemblies have marked certain milestones in the history of LWF. Often a "memorable event" or "moment of trial" or a particular style has captured the significance of an assembly. The First Assembly in Lund, 1947, is often described as "a defining moment in World Lutheranism." Delegates had come together without any pretense of providing an easy remedy for a broken world. Rather, they came seeking a united witness and a better medium for Lutheran cooperation and mutual assistance. Their decisions, as described by historian Richard Solberg, "gave distinction to the Lund Assembly far beyond its historic character as the First World Assembly of the Lutheran World Federation."[3]

Every delegate was aware of the terrible spiritual and physical devastation experienced by thousands upon thousands. James R. Crumley, Jr., who was a youth visitor to the Lund Assembly, recently said, "I will never get over seeing the suffering etched in so many faces." Many of the delegates came from nations that so recently had been at war with each other. But, as E. Theodore Bachmann commented in an essay, "Former enemy lines went into eclipse."[4] It was liberating to worship together at that First Assembly. Repentance, forgiveness, and reconciliation were at the heart of the worship experience.

There was a sense of urgency at that Assembly. With approximately ten million Lutheran refugees relief work was necessary. The urgency of the hour heightened the intention of the churches to take all possible steps, including cooperation with ecumenical and international relief organizations, to alleviate the suffering. A pattern was shaped for commitment to service, an enduring gift of the LWF over the past five decades, which included not only material and financial aid but also advocacy before the governments of the member churches and the United Nations and cooperation with other ecumenical and international organizations.[5] An important principle was established: aid to refugees had to be given without regard to origin, language, nationality, or status.

The sharing of human and material resources by member churches and the pioneering work in full-scale, highly organized programs created effective pathways for service. Such programs, now worldwide for both refugees and displaced persons, have remained at the heart of LWF's life and work. The concern for human rights, the need to address the root causes of social and economic injustice, and environmental issues are all part of the transformation of diaconal service over the years.

Space does not permit me to tell the story of this transformation as service programs shifted from Europe to the "Two-Thirds World." As new nations and new churches emerged as a consequence of decolonization, there grew an ever-broadening gap in socio-economic terms. This set a new framework for service. New contexts called for new concepts as traditional views of service based on compassion and charity clashed with concerns for community development and sustainable structures. Sharp questions were raised concerning the relationship between service, mission, and development, and the proclamation of the Gospel of Jesus Christ. In a world of cultural and religious pluralism, of social and political ambiguities, and of inequality in the distribution of resources all contributed to the transformation of service and to the question of how to carry it out responsibly.

Humanitarian needs remain enormous throughout the world today and LWF resources to ameliorate these needs are indeed small. But the tradition of commitment to service and the accomplishments of these fifty years continue to witness to the determination not to accept human suffering and pain and injustice as a given.

As change, adaptation, and transformation were necessary in diaconal service, so have they been necessary in LWF's involvement in mission as it moved from a free association of churches to a communion of churches. Some inter-Lutheran efforts to cooperate in mission pre-date the founding of LWF by at least a century. However, some tensions lingered from Lutheran World Convention activities at the founding of the LWF. There were signs of an inability to deal adequately with the question of cooperation in mission, as well as with the continuing need for assistance to "orphaned" missions who had been cut off from missionary leadership and mission board support since World War I.[6]

The 1947 Lund Assembly supported the priority of world mission as a cooperative task of Lutheran churches and mission agencies. The Assembly's vision for mission went considerably further than mission policies and practices followed at that time and had long-term consequences probably never imagined. The impulse for the vision came from the missionary character of the Gospel. The Assembly advocated a "unified approach of the Lutheran Church in its world mission."[7] Sending churches and mission societies were to consult, to take seriously their ecumenical obligations, to coordinate their policies, and to take steps toward the formation of nationwide, self-supporting Lutheran churches that would be able to carry forward the spreading of the Gospel. Orphaned mission fields were to be returned to their former supporting agencies as soon as possible. In the Lund vision, churches-- both the younger and the older-- were expected to recognize their partnership in a spirit of interdependence.

The consequences of this vision are the stories of LWF member churches developing new relationships, as autonomous churches began to move from dependence to partnership. The growing number of independent Lutheran churches which emerged from Africa and Asia and were accepted by the LWF as member churches challenged the traditional nineteenth-century practice of a one-directional missionary sending to receiving churches. The winds of change buffeted mission policies and practices of established churches as the younger churches "came of age," restive of being subject to mission policies decided by Western agencies and organizations. They wanted recognition as churches, a hearing of their own viewpoints and concerns about mission, and a chance for their leaders to have a place in planning and decision-making bodies. In many Western churches change surfaced as well in the working definition and theology of mission, showing the influence of the World Council of Churches in developing mission theology.

The fifth LWF Assembly in 1970 had to be moved from Brazil to France because of the political situation and the violation of human rights in Brazil. The impact of that Assembly on the Federation was greater than ever before and possibly since. Andre Appel, General Secretary at the time, observed that never before had the churches of Africa and Asia played such an active role in the Assembly.[8] The missionary theme for the fifth assembly, "Sent Into the World," and the change of venue raised both theological and ethical issues about the responsibility of the church in socio-political affairs. Assembly decisions again opened a new understanding of mission among member churches, namely mission as the task of the church in every place with evangelization at its center.[9] The Assembly's response to violations of human rights made it clear that prophetic witness for justice is an integral element of mission along with diaconal service and the sharing of spiritual and material resources.[10]

In the structural streamlining at Evian, all mission-related activities, which had been located in separate LWF units, were integrated into a unit designed as a forum and instrument of cooperation. A new title, Church Cooperation, was given to the Commission/Department, but not without extensive debate over the loss of the word "mission" in the title[11] (Twenty years later at the Curitiba Assembly in 1990, the word "mission" was restored in the title of the reorganized unit). In 1970 the intention was to recognize that every church, whether rich or poor, had something to give and to receive in fulfilling mission responsibilities in their home areas and also beyond their national boundaries. All churches were expected to be partners in a common global task of mission.

Following the Evian Assembly, mission and evangelism became important emphases.[12] Churches in the North and

South, East and West, were challenged by Assembly actions to evangelize within their specific contexts. Youth and women's gifts and concerns called for a more effective integration into LWF work. Mission was broadened to include the commitment to the struggle against racism, poverty, economic and social injustice, and a commitment to peace. The 1988 statement on mission, "Together in God's Mission," deepened the theological discussion on mission and evangelism both within the Federation and ecumenically. Mission understood as the "fundamental task of the church to participate in the whole mission of God to the whole world"[13] has turned the North-South axis of mission to a multi-form pattern where the life and witness of every church is to be regarded as a missionary act.

The recognition of the integrity of all member churches, especially the newly independent churches with their intent to find their own identity as the people of God and decide their own mission priorities and initiatives and interchurch relations, is the gift of the LWF to the communion of churches.

Fifty years—hardly a tick of time. Yet these fifty years have been extremely significant in Lutheran churches as they are coming together worldwide in service and mission.

Lutheran Communion in a Multi-cutural Identity

Musimbi Kanyoro

To think about one's identity in the framework of a celebration is a good thing. Paradoxically enough, one of our identities as Lutherans is that we are constantly and deeply engaged in the search for our identity. It often appears that we fear the real gist of Lutheranism will melt away, disappear in the sea of other denominations. Religious pluralism and multi-culturalism add to our concern over Lutheran identity. Alternatively, we truly are not sure of who we are, and we imagine that if we talk about it as often as possible, we might convince ourselves that we are Lutherans indeed.

As a first generation Lutheran, I am, frankly, perplexed and even impressed by the identity questions circulating among Lutherans. Ever since I started to read Lutheran theology and hang out with Lutherans, I discovered that there are three very important recipes for being a good Lutheran: First, it is very important to be Lutheran, and to say so in all places, and at all times and to all people. Second, it is okay to wonder what that really means. Third, it is a fine thing to continually research Lutheran identity to present public speeches on it, to convene discussion forums and, for future Lutherans, preserve all the research in books. I therefore find it proper and fitting to address this subject.

I was asked to address "Lutheran Identity in a multi-cultural communion." I was not comfortable with that. I shall address "Lutheran Communion in a multi-cultural identity." I have decided to reformulate the theme to allow myself to digress and to draw on my experience of the last ten years as an African with a global responsibility within the Lutheran World Federation. I could even have called this speech "The dilemma of an African who became Lutheran," or for that matter, "The adventures of an African Lutheran." Much has been written on the Lutheran identity issues.[1] I would like to contribute to this process by addressing issues which might be of concern to Lutherans from Africa. From time to time I have doubts about my Lutheran identity but for some reason I never seem to doubt that I am African!

Communion as the Globalization of Lutheranism

I recall with nostalgia the celebrations of the member churches of the federation during the Ninth Assembly in Hong Kong in 1997. I was privileged to be one of two hosts that evening. In addition to the beautiful sight of church leaders playing ball with balloons, I was privileged to interview some of the men and women who have been part of the LWF during the past 50 years. The participants illustrated the true image of the multi-culturalism of the Lutheran Communion, and the picturesque evening garnished by the theme of the Ninth Assembly, "In Christ—called to Witness," remains well documented in my mind's eye. Those multi-colored people of many nationalities who spoke many languages and were adorned in a variety of attire are the multi-cultural expression of the Lutheran Communion in various senses of the word.

We were all embraced by the crucified Christ, so beautifully shown to us on the Assembly poster designed by Dr. He Qi of the Nanjing Union Theological Seminary in China. The outstretched hands of the Crucified inviting the entire communion—this is the message around which we gathered for worship, business, and the jubilee celebration. In Hong Kong, the face of Christ was Chinese.

The delegates at the Ninth LWF Assembly understood themselves as Christians of the Lutheran confession at that particular moment in time situated in a Chinese context. Would the Lutheran Communion in the Chinese context impose an alien form of Christ upon this Asian gathering or would the Lutheran Communion use Asian culture forms in sharing Christ? The crucified Christ with a Chinese face was most appropriate. It is therefore in order to ask what it means to be Chinese Lutheran in China or Hong Kong? And how is that different from being a Chinese Lutheran living in Diaspora in Paris or San Francisco or Buenos Aires? How do these Lutherans differ from an African Lutheran in Namibia or a German Lutheran in Namibia? What exactly was peculiar to the gathering of diverse Lutherans at the jubilee assembly held in Hong Kong? When we Lutherans gather in one place, what is it that distinguishes us from one another, from other Christian Communions, from other Christians organized in diverse ways, such as Pentecostals, or, for that matter, from people of other faiths and commitments? Where are our similarities and differences, and what holds us together? It would be wonderful to respond to all the above questions, but I beg to be spared the speculation. Instead, let me reflect on what such questions might mean from my particular point of view.

The quest for identity takes a different stance. Lutheran churches perceive themselves as a "Communion" because such self-understanding demands a biblical vision of life together. A biblical vision calls for closeness without implying sameness. We are constantly reminded that "we who are many are one body in Christ" (Romans 12:5). The image of the Christian community as the Body of Christ, like many of the biblical images, is organic and relational. It conveys a strong sense of interdependence and an intrinsic potential for growth.

Images are an instructive and very effective means of communication. They don't merely illustrate something already well known , but images slightly disorient our conventional ways of understanding. The realistic and the unimaginable, are woven together in an unusual way. Images help us to imagine what is beyond the capacity of language and expound on what does not fully correspond to any reality we have experienced. One could argue that this is the eschatological dimension of language.

Is there any way to maintain the concern for communion in such images while dismantling their reflection of an unjust social system? Is it possible to renew such images from alternative experiences in diverse cultures? Can we develop a fair balance of power, true reciprocity and exclusivity so that interdependence is not perverted into constantly new forms of exploitation? And if so, how can reconciliation occur without the victim paying the cost? How do we taste and glimpse in our lives the Reign of God as we seek to be a communion in our diversity? These are but some of the questions we could explore together in the communion as we continue to take responsibility for who we are and who we might become.

The Unfinished Dimension of Becoming a Communion

The Bible provides many powerful images of the God-given communion. If we translate the Greek word "koinonia" as communion, we may also understand such word as meaning "participation and solidarity." In this sense communion is that which happens when people find a new focus in relationships and begin to live a common history of freedom for others. In whatever way this commonness will find meaningful expression, Active participation in a common purpose is decisive. a communion has no one single social form. It has to be spelt out in the available groupings and cultural forms of each society. Communication happens through culture, hence, culture determines the shape of the communion. In the New Testament, the word "koinonia" (which translates as communion), is used in connection with a new focus on relationships that comes from the sharing of a common history with Jesus. The early Christians had a common share in the life of Jesus. Thus, in 1 Corinthians 10:16-17, Paul speaks of the act of breaking bread as a participation or koinonis.

> "The cup of blessing which we bless is not a participation in the blood of Christ? The bread which we break, is it not a participation in the body of Christ? Because there is one bread we who are many are one body for we all partake of one bread. . ."

When we explore our identity as a Lutheran Communion in a multi-cultural context, we are really speaking about a common participation in the gifts of God and solidarity with one another in our common service in the society. Our credibility or communion is called to question when we are not present with people in their quests to realize their dignity. Participation is not about liberalism but about liberation. To move from a federation to a communion requires that we assume more accountability from and with each other as churches in the communion. A jubilee celebration must send us forth to explore the depth and breadth of the question of how to address assumptions of superiority and inferiority which have been historically implanted in our attitudes towards one another and which have hindered the participation of all. This newfound identity from a federation to a communion [2] has to be seen in the context of *oikoumene.*

Confessional Lutherans must be conscientiously committed to membership in both evangelical and ecumenical movements within one Church catholic. Our quest for a Lutheran Communion cannot be replaced or even separated from the more urgent quest for visible unity among all Christian churches which confess Jesus Christ as God and savior according to the Scriptures and therefore seek to be obedient together to their common calling. In the Bible, Oikoumene refers to the whole-inhabited earth. All the human groupings in the world are part of God's house (oikos) and are participants in God's economics (*oikonomia*). It was to this world that the good news of God's love in Jesus Christ was addressed. The words of Matthew 24:14 remind us of this universal concern.

> "And this gospel of the kingdom will be preached throughout the whole world as a testimony to all nations and then the end will come."

In the history of the church, the *oikoumene* gradually came to mean the Christian world; the ecumenical focus shifted from mission to the preservation of the purity, unity, and orthodoxy of the church. In modern times, our understanding of *oikoumene* has again broadened as we discover the many human groupings and different faiths found in the global village. Hence, when we speak of communion today in the context of the *oikoumene,* we emphasize the importance of unity in service to the needs of the world created by God. In our concern for the *oikoumene* and the liberation of all people in the world, we are constantly challenged by the difficulties of working together.

Globalization: a Challenge to the Communion.

Theologian Thomas Thangaraj says,

> "One definition of globalization is the elimination of distance. In the present mission context we are being brought close to one another. The elimination of distance has serious economic, political and religious implications."[3]

Lutheranism has been global, which is partially due to the missionary history of the Christian faith. The history of the church is predicated on the concept of a global church. The apostolic mandate for mission in the Gospel of Matthew (28:18-20) challenges all Christians to share the good news of Jesus with others in their own "homes" and beyond their geographical boundaries. Hence, I think communion means to seek to understand our Christian task of being people of God in the world. To be in the world means to get involved in God's love affair with the world. The bible says "For God so loved the world. . ." (John 3:16). It is in loving the world that the son of God was sent to us. The Bible does not say "For God so loved the Church." The work of the church is simply to be part of the world and to continue God's love for the world. Our identity in our various contexts will become clearer as we love the world around and beyond us. Letty Russell tells this story of the former archbishop of the Church of Sweden and long-time Professor of Theology at Harvard Divinity School, Krister Stendahl.

"Many years ago I heard Krister Stendahl quote a rabbinical saying that theology is worrying about what God is worrying about when God gets up in the morning. It would seem to Stendahl, that God is worrying about the mending of creation trying to straighten up the mess so that the groaning creation will be set free."[4]

What happens to the communion when we all go about loving the world? How do we do this loving? It would seem to me we could say to each other that to be Lutheran is to seek to live in community with one another across barriers of gender, race, religion, or confession, class, caste, or lifestyle. We could publicly acknowledge that to choose to do so involves a continuous struggle, not only to discover our identity, but also to face the contradictions between what we say and what we are able to do. The world is so much with us that the contradictions we face in seeking to underline our identity as a Lutheran Communion seem minor in relation to contradictions of poverty and affluence, the exploitation of persons and natural resources, and the resulting indifference and apathy that continue to mark our reaction to the suffering around us. Illnesses such as AIDS and other social and personal contradictions which challenge us nationally and globally also bear on the nature of talking about church. To sort out these contradictions by acknowledging that they are part of our unfinished agenda gives us a certain freedom to continue living together in the context of contradictions. The quest for identity as a Lutheran Communion is a challenge that should always be with us. It is part of our legitimate unfinished business.

We need a disturbing agenda, an agenda that will make us want to meet and put our heads together in worship as a visible sign of our global nature. First, is it not enough to celebrate our identity in Christ? Elements of the Lutheran liturgy, reformation songs, the catechisms, etc., have held us together and will continue to do so! Second, we need to meet to exchange ideas on how the Lutheran Communion accommodates and nurtures its multi-cultural encounters. To see each other, to share meals, words, and even frustrations is an indication of solidarity. Third, we need to meet to check out puzzling matters. For example, my small home church, the Evangelical Lutheran Church in Kenya, recently acquired the status of having bishops rather than presidents. It was very important for our bishop that the bishop of the North Western Diocese of the Evangelical Lutheran Church in Tanzania be the one to install him, the reason being that the bishop of Arusha, our geographical neighbor did not quite have it right. I mean the apostolic succession. This interesting phenomenon appears time and again, even with our dialogue partners. A number of churches choose to have bishops to gain the respect of other churches around them, and, as if that were not enough, our bishops are now divided into those who have it and those who don't. Then there is another phenomenon: The Hungarian and the Latvian ministers have it. But when I was traveling with one of the Hungarian pastors in Latvia, the archbishop of Latvia did not recognize her ministry. We need to meet regularly in order to talk about such confusing matters.

Our History: A Challenge to the Communion

The time has come to stop riding on the mistakes of the past and to begin envisioning a future that utilizes the learning of the past. While it is necessary to recognize that the cultural invasion of the 19-century missionary church was traumatic to the people of other geographical and cultural contexts, we have been angry and ever resentful about the erosion of our dignity and self-worth by a Christianity in foreign attire. The resulting identity crisis is still felt in our churches, and if we do not talk about it, it can be a hindrance to becoming a communion. Our anger must now be put to good use. People from former mission-sending countries need to accept the consequences of history, but they must now move on from the paralysis produced by the guilt of imperialism that accompanied the spread of the Church. We all now need to ask the question that the young rich ruler asked Jesus: "Good teacher, what must I do to inherit eternal life?" (Luke 18:18).

Lutheran theology and dogma has taught us to value the need for grace. I think all Lutherans agree that we are sinners in need of the grace of God. To be in communion, therefore, as we are, is to know how to ask for forgiveness and then to proceed and get done what must be done. The major task of our churches is to teach us once again how to pray "forgive us our trespasses as we forgive those who trespass against us."

Many sisters and brothers who visit churches in Africa, Asia-Pacific, and Latin America are disappointed that we sing the songs and use liturgies of the 15th century Europe. Some of us share disappointment and discomfort and do not always feel at home in our own churches, especially when we come in contact with the ecumenical movement where so much change has taken place. But I think when our churches in the South sing old German tunes, we must affirm that those songs have become a mark of our Lutheran identity. Lutherans all over the world sing "Á Mighty Fortress" and as much as the imagery in the song does not speak well in a world where the church should focus on images of peace rather than war, these elements of the Lutheran faith have managed to penetrate the multi-cultural world where Lutheranism is found. Those elements of worship link us to the global Lutheranism and also distinguish us from Baptists and Catholics, Anglicans, etc.

Identity is more than a piece of cloth, that you put on in the morning and change in the evening. Some northern Lutheran churches have begun to learn African and Asian and Pacific and Latin American songs. The struggle of singing other people's music will eventually become mutual, and that will lessen the identity gap. If we are to take issues of identity seriously, we must accept that our past and present are interwoven and will always interact.

To be a communion implies that there must be room for those for whom theology from Germany cannot be the only one to determine the paths of the communion. The identity of Lutheran churches as a communion gives churches in the South the legitimacy to claim mutuality, which can only be realized in participation and solidarity with the total life of the communion. It gives the identity of Lutheran churches in the North the opportunity to relinquish some of their power, a power that has often been expressed in theology, economics, and intellectual domination. With our eyes focused on life in the communion, it becomes more than urgent for us to explore how we express mutuality in the communion. How do we welcome and value each and every person, each and every church, and each and every community's gifts at the common table of the communion? What do we look like when we share what we have in common? How do we celebrate our new identity? Is it even possible? Is it possible to grasp the same images of communion and the same visions of unity across differences imposed by injustice? How does the imbalance of power influence our understanding of church history, church polity, and Scripture? As we speak of belonging to a communion, we also reveal our dreams and tell how we envision what living together will be like when God's purpose for the whole creation is fulfilled.

Contextual Pluralism: A Challenge to the Communion

Our lives together for the last 50 years through the LWF have been significant and meaningful. To celebrate the Lutheran World Federation's continuing evolvement as a communion on five continents is a sign of progress. This could also be a time to bring fresh and contemporary meaning to the concept of world communion while recognizing our special peculiarities. How may we express our social, historical, and continued reformation, which has allowed our self-understanding as a Federation to grow into the understanding of ourselves as a communion? In our search for new ways to live out our communion and to express our solidarity with one another throughout the world let us reflect on how the concept of communion may be challenged in different multi-cultural contexts. I will present some scenarios that concern me as an African Lutheran.

Secular Religion: A Challenge to the Communion
Lutheranism in Nordic Countries

Iceland, Norway, Sweden, Denmark, and Finland are usually grouped together as like-minded pluralistic societies.

They share much in terms of culture, economy, social order, and the Lutheran church as an established state church. In addition, Swedes, Danes, and Norwegians share mutually intelligible languages, and Icelanders can use Danish as a medium. The Nordic countries became Lutheran with the Reformation of the 16th century; since then their constitutions have incorporated the state-church system with the head of the state also being the head of the church. This system, in which the state is involved in the decision-making of the church, has remained something of a mystery and is sometimes critiqued by other Lutherans inside and outside of the Nordic countries. The issues are not as simple as stated above but the above background will do for my case.

Participating in the LWF study on *Communion, Community and Society,* Pedersen presents a study of the Danish State-church. She notes that while the Danish State-church records millions of members, only a handful actually go to church, and although the existing churches are mostly empty, Danes continue to build more churches. There are even suggestions that the empty churches could be "turned into arts or community centers." [5]

Questions are often asked in the communion: When we talk of numbers in representation or a base for common decision making in the communion, can we really continue to give preference to countries in which the numbers of church-going Christians has so much diminished? Is this practical, fair, and just? Similarly, does this phenomenon call for a reverse missionary endeavor, and should it be a concern of the whole communion? Is it the task of the communion to discuss and to agree that the Nordic countries are new mission fields in need of the attention and concern of the whole communion? But if the churches in the communion want to assist the Nordic countries in mission work, with whom do they discuss the matter? Mission societies, the Church of Norway, the government, or all of the above? In Norway, the government and the king are involved in the appointment of the majority of the clergy, including all deans and bishops. Are African governments to be invited to this debate in Africa? Norwegian Lutheranism of Norway is known mostly through missionaries sent by missionary societies. When African church leaders visit Norway at the invitation of the missionaries, they often do not meet their counterparts, i.e. the bishops of Norway, unless special arrangements have been made or they are directly on a mission with the Church of Norway. Since African churches that relate to the mission agencies are in communion with the Church of Norway, should the mission agencies not collaborate with each other and have something to do with each other and with the church of Norway in order to enhance the concept of communion?

Let us look at another Nordic scenario. There are ongoing discussions of changes forthcoming in Sweden, that will separate church and state. While some people welcome the changes, I have also heard worries that the church of Sweden may not have so much access to government money in the future and thus might not be able to maintain identity as a donor church within the communion (by way of North-South relationship). How shall we in Africa relate to the Church of Sweden when it can no longer support the Evangelical Lutheran Church in Zimbabwe, South Africa, Tanzania, and others?

Gunnar Staalsett[6] gave many speeches to prepare the church for the discussion and the vote on the identity as "Communion" before the eighth LWF assembly. At the African regional meeting in Madagascar in 1987, he spoke on "Lutheran Communion in the African Context." In the presentation, Staalsett analyzed the political conflicts and the poverty in Africa as the context through which the churches of Africa live out their communion. He notes that "the Church is growing faster in Africa and in some parts of Asia (China and South Korea) than anywhere else."[7] Staalett's observations remain valid in 1998. They have been reinforced by the conflicts on the Great Lakes region and by other issues afflicting the continent of Africa. If it's time that the continent is becoming more Christianized and at the same time more pauperized or impoverished, then we are in for more trouble.

African churches will only continue to participate as channels of Church Aid to Northern church agencies. Church historian Mugambi predicts: "If systemic affluence in the North is associated with secularism and systemic poverty in Africa is associated with Christianity in the 21st century, Christianity will rapidly lose its popularity in tropical Africa."[8] Mugambi's prediction is supported by the fact that in Africa, people with financial means are often not the strongest church attendants. There are signs of secularism's in urban Africa and among the western educated elites.

If we take communion seriously, Africa and Europe must both go to Asia to learn from those churches that had to survive without the help of Europe or America because of the war. Under Japanese occupation, missionaries from countries in conflict with Japan had to leave, but the church continued with leadership provided by local Christians. The recent opening of China has also shown how a people committed to identity with Jesus is sustained through the unknown, even in a context of irreverence toward religion.

Religious Pluralism:
A Challenge to the Communion of Churches in Asia

Religious pluralism and its theological and ecclesiological implications form an important theme of identity questions. At the ninth LWF assembly on July 14, the delegates had a chance to experience this pluralism through perspective presentations from Buddhist, Muslim, and Confucian representatives. As part of the multi-faith encounter, Dr. Paul V. Martinson invited the assembly to think about "what basing one's existence upon the story of Jesus Christ might mean today for those who are Lutherans in our interaction with people and communities of other distinctive commitments?"

While this question tells the true story of the daily life of Asian Lutheran churches, multi-faith connections are now needed all over the world. Our Christian identity as rooted in Jesus Christ is also our strongest affirmation of pluralism and openness. Beyond all sectarianism, the life of Jesus stands as a solid reminder of one who was always present for others.

His love was for all humankind. In Jesus we see God showing no partiality. This stance is by no means an invitation to affirm secularism or religious neutrality, for to do so would be to lose the identity with the one who constantly calls people to more than mere friendship. Our identity involves sharing God's hospitality, which is offered through the salvation that Christ the Savior offers to all of humanity. The church cannot escape the haunting question of "how can one talk about Christ in a pluralistic society?" The churches in Asia must share with the whole communion their experiences in a multi-religious context.

How then do we define syncretism today? Is heaven really reserved only for people who think and behave in a certain uniform way? Do the creeds and scriptures of the Christian church mark the limit of God's grace? Can we, having full knowledge and an expanded awareness of the variety of religious expressions, insist on yesterdays religious exclusiveness? These questions are not only difficult to an-swer; but for the institutional church, they are difficult to face. How is the institutional church to deal with the seeming hopelessness and relativity that is a result of this dilemma. Should the institutional church admit the Christianity might, after all, hold only partial truth.

Local Congregations and Communities: A Challenge to the Communion of Latin American Churches

To listen to the voices of the laity in the communion is no longer a romantic exploration, but food for the communion. Take for example, the Lutheran church in Brazil. One might ask how it has been shaped by the experiences of the *communidades de base* (Base communities) and what its new self-understanding (if any) might mean to the rest of the communion. The whole Latin American experience during the dirty wars, the consequent struggle for democracy, and the new conscientization of reading the Bible with the eyes of the poor and the marginalized, could offer a different way of interpreting the formula "Justification by Faith" so loved by Lutherans. How can such a formula be relevant in a world where people are degraded to subhuman standards and the rich dominate over the poor? The option for the poor is fundamental and of immediate relevance to the world in which we live today, unlike traditional Lutheran theology which often remains the luxury of the few academics. Yet to say it so plainly would seem to neglect the shortcomings that are in new theologies. The contradictions within and around us have to do with the inconsistencies between the way we experience reality and the way our faith has been shaped over time by theology, doctrine, and dogma.

Cultures and Traditions: A Challenge to the Communion. Indigenous Peoples of the World

The communion will be all the richer if the participation of new players brings something new to the table. The churches continue to fear exploring what cultures and traditions might offer to the communion. Yet the identity of the communion would be incomplete if the communion were not able to say; that the Lutheran communion is a *Dalit, San or Same* communion, to name but a few. At the World Conference on Mission and Evangelism held in Salvador, Bahia, Brazil, (November 1997) the indigenous people cried out for recognition by the churches. They argued that God was present prior to church and that they brought an experience of God with them to the church that did not originate in Christianity but in different cultures and traditions. They stated that indigenous people have often experienced the church as a destructive force and stressed that the gospel is never available to people unless it is embodied in particular cultures.[9] People's cultures and traditions are the strongest seats of their identity. Is there no possibility to imagine a cultural Christianity that is truly liberating to every convert?

The experiences of women continue to pose alternative questions to culture. When is culture liberating and when is it not? Women in Africa, for example, reject the use of culture that is harmful to their health and to the health of female children. In my writings, including a presentation to the aforementioned mission conference, I have argued that culture needs to be put to the test in order to prove its liberation potential before it is wholly embraced. Female circumcision, child marriages, and several food and blood taboos imposed on women are some of the causes which invite such critique.

Women and Gender Issues: A Challenge to the Communion.

During my ten-year tenure as a program secretary for Women in Church and Society in the LWF, I learned that there are many subtle ways for communities to sustain monologues rather than dialogues on the question of gender. More often that not, gender considerations are already distinguished by the inequalities that exist in the particular communities. Inequality is the first obstacle to any kind of partnership and participation. Gender inequalities manifest themselves in different ways, such as disparities in opportunities, a lack of access to resources, education, an absence or scarcity of women in the decision making, etc. Many of the above-mentioned issues are usually explained by resorting to culture as the dictate for injustice to women. For this reason, the word gender is used. Gender analysis seeks to examine the situation of both men and women and to correct the inherent cultural injustice to either. Churches in the communion can accompany one another in speaking out for liberating changes for women; to shy away from having practices and cultures that promote violence and death to women and girls has no justification whatsoever.

The Lutheran Communion has made great strides by opening up the ordained ministry to both men and women. The presence of women bishops in the communion speaks louder that words. But the ordination of women is still the most sensitive and sometimes compromising issue in the communion. Churches that ordain women often prefer not to be seen as influencing other churches. When situations of conflict arise with women from non-ordaining churches, they get most support from women while the leaders of the churches tend to keep quiet and assume silent diplomacy, a diplomacy which is used when the communion holds discussions with churches that do not ordain women. On such occasions, women are only included with great caution and it is rare that women are asked to take a lead role even if they qualify to do so. Thus, the communion sends out different messages to its dialogue partners.

Some in the communion have equated the non-ordination of women to apartheid in the church and have advocated a "status confessionis." I tested this option with women from the affected churches and a majority were opposed, including those seeking ordination. They felt that with or without ordination they wanted to know that they were worshipping members of their churches. The ordination of women will remain in the discussion of the communion for a long time to come.

Third World Theologies: Challenges to the Communion.

During the last three decades, the people of the South have found new ways of talking religion. We have seen the rise and the blossoming of various theologies and theologizing groups. They have strongly challenged their mothers and fathers of faith by declaring that Europe and America are not really the cradle of the world. According to these "third world, third eye" theologies, the West has no right to make carbon copies out of their people in the name of a Christian conversion or theology. Occasionally, resistance of missionized people is stated as a matter of fact: "We refuse to serve simply as raw material which offers use for their salvation."[9] At one time this frankness was shocking to traditional missionary agencies and to the Churches of Europe and America who were not well prepared for the new consciousness of the South and its articulating voicing of this rejection. Today the issues of identity really hinge on the initiatives of different peoples to have their differences affirmed. That is, difference must not always be seen to be a problem and should not be made into a problem. Rather, difference is a reality and can function in a creative and mutually supportive way. To affirm difference is to be open to what that difference might bring to relationships, systems, and structures. The search to have one's difference affirmed is a continuous search in all persons for what we might become when we relate in just ways to each other and to all that is created by God, the creator of difference. The critique of European theologies and Lutheranism is a necessary step toward communion. That does not exclude the critiques of Southern theologies but it puts the emphasis on where change must first occur. The communion of churches has to take the task of being a conciliar community, and thus to bear the identity of the church as the one body with many parts.

The Unfinished Business of Reconciliation.

The LWF is a place where dialogue and fruitful encounters are possible. The globalization of Lutheranism makes possible new identities and a new solidarity among all Lutherans, North and South alike. Koinonia is a complex concept of interdependence and exchange, diversity and unity; it is static and dynamic; complete and at the same time still in the process of becoming. Every community should review its own structures to see if everyone has equal opportunity to contribute according to his or her gifts. This review must happen in a process of dialogue, in which awareness of the other becomes part of one's own identity. Diversity between and among churches and individuals is to be expected and celebrated. In the words of theologian Letty Russell,

"We all have to put on new glasses to be able to understand the many communities who come together as Christ's body. Each person speaks in a different language, lives out the burdens of a different political and economic system and thinks in widely different ways about ministry, leadership and all the rest. Some sing and others drum and others dance. It is in the struggle to listen and understand and "to love one another with mutual affection" (Rom: 12:10) that lives are transformed and connected in new ways"[10]

Response to Musimbi Kanyoro

José David Rodriguez

Dr. Musimbi Kanyoro, with discernment, and humor,
raises very important issues about the past, present, and
future work of the Lutheran World Federation. She raises
important challenges, exciting opportunities, and a very
positive vision of hope for the future. For that reason, my role
in responding aims not to question these challenges, opportunities, and the hope, but to support them and to move them
forward. It is also an opportunity to initiate a dialogue in the
hope that others from a variety of perspectives, experience,s
and visions of hope will join us with their questions, gifts and
enthusiasm.

Most of the concerns raised by Kanyoro are very dear to
me. As a product of the missionary work that celebrates this
year a century of Lutheran work in Puerto Rico, I have also
struggled to make sense of my identity as Lutheran and
Latino. In so doing, I have tried to understand myself not in
the context of an already defined religious identity that wit-
nesses to a multicultural communion, but from the perspective of a Lutheran Communion in which my contribution is as
important as that of others in our common effort to bring
meaning and witness to our religious and spiritual vocation.
Kanyoro's contribution as a Lutheran from Africa is not just
relevant for those who come from Africa or happen to live in
that country. That it is, of course. But her contribution is also
important to the community of believers in our common
effort to witness to the Gospel as a reformation movement
within the Church Catholic that cuts across the boundaries of
time and space, of language and culture, of gender and class,
and many other barriers created by humankind. Kanyoro's
right to witness within this Communion stands or falls not
with the recognition of what Lutherans from Europe and the
United States might provide. Rather it has the same basis that

gave Martin Luther in the 16th century not just the right, but also the calling to make a public witness to the Gospel in responding to the challenges, which faced his brothers and sisters in Germany in their common effort to be faithful to the Gospel.

Kanyoro, does not need and official recognition of her status as a *bona fide* Lutheran to make her point, but, as many Latino students in this seminary remind me, in this country it is best to be documented in case you have to face *la migra*, representatives of the INS (Immigration and Naturalization Service). In order to avoid any kind of misunderstanding or problem now and during the celebration of this conference, I publicly state that she is duly recognized as a Lutheran in full communion with those of us coming from the island of Puerto Rico.

Kanyoro, argues that the multicultural identity of the Lutheran communion is already taking place. One sees evidence of this multicultural identity in the presence of people of many colors from many nationalities, who speak many languages and are adorned in a variety of attires at international assemblies like the one gathered in Hong Kong in 1997 for worship, business and celebration. One sees evidence in the decision of this 9th Assembly of the LWF in Hong Kong to change its self-understanding from being a Federation to becoming a communion.

Kanyoro explores the implications of becoming a communion and the challenges we face to meet this goal on a local, national, and international level. By focusing on the biblical witness, the wisdom of God's self-revelation, and the marvelous eschatological dimension of language, she challenges us with a renewed vision and calls us to commit ourselves in solidarity with one another and to respond to the needs of our brothers and sisters. "We need a disturbing agenda," she states, "an agenda that will make us want to meet and put our heads together to pursue the business of involving ourselves in God's love affair in the world." These are powerful words, words that not only describe what is happening now, but also remind us that that which is and will take place needs our contribution, our participation, our willingness to join together in this endeavor. While Kanyoro places this task in the context of God's redeeming gifts and empowerment for this calling, the fact remains that there is some unfinished business to which we need to attend. This communion will take place as we make it our own and strive to share it with others. It is in this context that I raise the following questions:

As we seek to participate in this communion:

How do we discern the gifts to be employed in moving forward the agenda of our Lutheran communion, given the fact that these gifts differ and that they need to be complemented with those of others? When are we called to exert a prophetic role, to be in solidarity with those who need our support, our gifts and our presence? Kanyoro makes reference to this issue. I would like to expand her thoughts a little further. Who gets angry first? Who begins the process of forgiveness and reconciliation?

When and how do we get angry at each other? How do we develop a common *safe* ground to differ from each other, to confront each other, to affirm and support each other, not to transcend our God-given differences, but to use them constructively in order to stimulate the best from our partners and ourselves in this common task?

How do we prioritize the tasks to be carried out with those with whom we share this task when our different voices are not heard in the same way, when our languages need translation, not just to a common language, but to a commonality of experiences that manifest conflict, prejudice, and the wounds in our historical background? How do we do this in such a way that there might be a common affirmation of our God—given dignity, as well as a better stewardship of the resources available?

Since we don't all come at the same time to this communion nor with the same gifts, how can we join in the task of developing a process that may enhance our ability to work together and support our efforts mutually?

Kanyoro provides valuable hints and introduces stimulating suggestions in addressing these and similar matters. As I mentioned earlier, the goal of my questions is to continue to stimulate this conversation to provide content to these provocative challenges, opportunities, and visions of hope.

Kanyoro shares with us her eloquent expression of motivation, commitment, and vision. I hope our willingness to join hands in these efforts, as we celebrate 50 years of service of the Lutheran World Federation in North America, will also serve as an stimulus for others to become part of this communion of faith in moving forward the witness of love to our brothers and sisters in the world.

Communion and Interfaith Relationships
The Challenge of a "New Ecumenism"

J. Paul Rajashekar

A satisfactory approach to our theme hinges on how we define the concept of "communion," whether narrowly or broadly, institutionally or theologically, sociologically or ecclesiologically; and on how we discern the nature and character of "interfaith relationships" in the divergent social and cultural contexts of our world. Bearing in mind the context of this celebration marking the 50th Anniversary of the Lutheran World Federation (LWF), two avenues of exploration seem pertinent.

The first and the most obvious interpretation of "communion" is that it refers to the LWF as an institution, an instrument of Lutheran confessional communion around the world. In this sense, our exploration of the theme involves an analysis of the evolution of LWF's involvement in issues of other faiths in its institutional history, including the deliberations in Commissions and Assemblies on this theme. A retrospective analysis of this kind may be appropriate and insightful on this occasion. Second, the term "communion" could be explored in a more technical or theological sense, as referring to an evolving self-understanding within the Lutheran confessional family. Understood from this point of view, our theme calls for a critical reflection on the implications of interfaith relationships for our emerging ecclesiology. An analysis of this nature may be of value for future theological deliberations in the Lutheran communion.

By restricting the topic to these two avenues of inquiry, I have specifically chosen not to address issues pertaining to the nature and character of inter-religious dialogue and relations today or crucial themes in contemporary theology of religions from a Lutheran standpoint. I refer you to the literature on those issues, including some published by the Lutheran World Federation.[1] Those issues undoubtedly have a bearing on our analysis and will become somewhat explicit in my discussion in the second part of this paper.

I. Federation and Interreligious Relations

I believe that the theme "Communion and Interfaith Relationships" was chosen for discussion on this occasion primarily because of its potential to become a major concern for Christian churches around the world in the next millennium, and not because interfaith concerns have in any way shaped or guided LWF's ecclesiological discussions. In fact, interreligious questions have been a marginal concern, at best, in much of LWF's history. It was only during the last two decades that concerns related to people of other faiths were even recognized on the agenda of LWF. Lutherans in general and the LWF in particular have been extremely cautious and reluctant to take up interreligious issues, even after Vatican II and the World Council of Churches (WCC) had come to recognize the significance of the issues posed by religious pluralism. There seems to be two major factors that account for this hesitation: (1) cultural and (2) missiological. A cursory look at the LWF history, I hope, may help substantiate this observation.

Cultural Captivity.

The famous or infamous discussion on "Justification" at the Fourth Assembly at Helsinki in 1963 is an interesting entry point that in a way lifts up the LWF's general attitude toward issues of non-Western or non-Christian cultures in its early history. The first draft of the document (No. 75) on "Justification" began with an analysis of the human situation. The draft characterized the human situation by using a typically

Barthian phrase "godlessness."[2] Given the theological climate of the post-war era, the pervasive awareness of secularism and the secularization process at work in many Western countires, and the emergence of Marxism as a powerful ideology in Eastern Europe, the phrase "godlessness" made much sense to the drafters of the document. Interestingly, in the ensuing plenary discussion, a lone voice from India, Dr. P. David, a professor of Hinduism, spoke supporting the motion to refer the document to a small committee with the following remarks:

I am going to say that this small group should take into account this fact: that the statement in this document involves utterances that godlessness is prevailing all over. And it is true. As Christians we accept this. But I make two reservations. One is, there are certain religions and countries which do not accept this statement. Particularly, the principle of godlessness would not apply to a country like India where people are intensely religious. Such a situation should also be reflected. And the other observation I would make is: secularism is prevailing in the western world. The term "godlessness" has also been applied to this secularized world. I would like to see the meaning of God revealed in Jesus Christ be more prominently brought out as an interpretation in this statement. Otherwise "godlessness" would be challenged.[3]

This plea of a theologian from a non-Christian culture was of course ignored in the subsequent version of the document and in the final version that was approved by the Commission on Theology following the Assembly.[4] The phrase "godlessness" was retained as an universal description of the human situation of the 1960s.

I cite this rather obscure and isolated reference drawn from an Assembly debate to illustrate the theological and cultural insensitivity among the theologians who shaped the early history of the Federation. This should hardly surprise anyone. It was still a period when the consciousness of religious plurality had not been adequately understood in LWF member churches. Among the three dominant blocks of

Lutherans in the LWF, the Nordic and German Lutherans had yet to experience religious plurality in their midst, which was to come with immigrants a decade or so later. The third block, consisting of North American Lutherans, had not yet foreseen the impact of the Asian Immigration Act of 1965 that opened the door for Asian immigrants to American shores. Helsinki discussions, furthermore, were carried on under the methodology of "classical theology" which tended to either dismiss issues of other faiths and cultures as irrelevant or, in all probability, operated under certain *a priori* theological judgments about other faiths within the framework of the Lutheran tradition. It must be noted, however, that the theologians at Helsinki were more preoccupied with foundational questions about Lutheran confessional identity in the modern world. Perhaps they were more frustrated by the lack of consensus among Lutherans on such a vital matter as the doctrine of justification on which "the church stands or falls," and hence were unwilling to be sidetracked by issues that were thought to be not so central to the life and theology of the Northern block of Lutheran Churches. This point, in a way, was conceded in a review done in 1962 that noted "the work of the Department of Theology has been concentrated chiefly in Europe and North America."[5]

The official history of the LWF, *From Federation to Communion*, is fairly accurate in noting that from the time of the Fifth Assembly in Evian in 1970 LWF began to show an openness towards issues arising from the "two-thirds world." Theology in the LWF in the 70s had entered a phase of "prophetic denunciation."[6] As a consequence, classical methodological approaches to theology had begun to give way to contextual reflections on issues, such as social justice, human rights, apartheid, peace, sexism, and other ideological themes. The so called "Self-Studies" or "ecclesiological studies" conducted in a variety of socio-cultural contexts in the 70s, generated some significant social and political issues with reference to the Lutheran doctrine of "Two Kingdoms," and precipitated tensions and controversy within the LWF. But striking in retrospect is how little attention these studies paid to religious and cultural questions. The focus was primarily and invariably on Lutheran social and political responsibility and other ideological questions. These were, by and large, unresolved issues or even neuralgic themes from Lutheran history in Europe, now being sorted out in cooperation with and in relation to churches from the South.

The point becomes clear to anyone who reads the controversial book by Ulrich Duchrow, *Conflict Over The Ecumenical Movement.* This book leaves the unmistakable impression that the ecclesiological studies of the 70s in the LWF were fundamentally concerned with intra-European squabbles or conflicts about social and political responsibility between neo-confessionalists and radical activists in relation to the structures of LWF and the WCC.[7] There is no denial that these studies had profound implications for the churches in the South and, in effect, promoted their active participation in LWF's deliberations. Nonetheless, issues of religious and cultural nature were either ignored or received little attention in these studies.

The final report of the contextual studies collected together in *The Identity of the Church and Its Service to the Whole Human Being* (1977) includes a section on "The Context of Pluralistic Cultures" which lifts up the problems of folk churches in former GDR and Finland, the problem of leisure time in Sweden, the issue of middle class in United States, and the ideology of Ujamaa in Tanzania.[8] The focus on ideological studies related to "Marxism and China" and "Movements of Social Change in Various Cultural Contexts" remains remarkably silent on religio-cultural issues.[9] In the 70s, despite a shift in methodology from classical to contextual and from deductive to inductive, LWF's sensitivity to issues of non-Christian cultures or of other faiths is not self-evident, excepting where the consultations pertain to Lutheran relations with Jewish people, again a European problem not unrelated to issues of Lutheran political responsibility.[10]

It was at the Dar-e-Salaam Assembly in 1977 that questions of other faiths appeared on the agenda of the LWF, influenced in part by the rise of resurgent Islam and its growing prominence in the continent of Africa, and partly due to the appearance of new religious movements in North Atlantic Countries. At Dar-e-Salaam, it was resolved that the question of relations with Jewish people be distinguished from issues pertaining to all other faiths and to keep them separate forever. The Assembly also recommended that studies be undertaken pertaining to traditional cultures,[11] new religious movements, and "theological understandings of practical relations with people of other faiths." The resolutions of the Assembly encouraged studies but refrained from suggesting actual dialogue with people of other faiths except that resources pertaining to dialogue be made available to churches.[12] This implicit reticence toward interreligious dialogue is noteworthy. By the time Lutherans met in Dar-e-Salaam, Vatican II had already issued "The Declaration on the Relationship of the Church to Non-Christian Religions" (*Nostra Aetate* in 1965), a significant document in Christian history. Also, the WCC in 1971 had established a new Sub-Unit on Dialogue with people of Other Faiths, thus highlighting interreligious dialogue as a major concern of the churches. The debate about interreligious dialogue that occurred at the Nairobi Assembly of the WCC in 1975, seems to have had no spillover effect on the LWF Assembly. Lutheran fears about dealing with other faiths and issues of other cultures remained intact at this point and became more pronounced at the Seventh Assembly at Budapest in 1984.

The issue was dealt as a sub-section of "Mission and Evangelism" at Budapest. Again, the Assembly resolutions treated other faiths as matters for further study. LWF was urged—note the cautious language—"to explore the possibilities of and means of developing face to face encounters with people of other faiths at different levels of church life in order to learn about other faiths and to communicate the gospel."[13] Of course, the word "dialogue" was studiously avoided and the phrase "face to face encounter" implied a confrontational approach. Judging on the basis of various Budapest resolutions, the focus on other faiths at the Assembly was not because of Lutheran sensitivity to issues in the life of churches in non-Christian or non-Western cultures. The concern, rather, emerged primarily on account of perceived fears about the growth of new religious movements from the East in North Atlantic Countries and their growing influence upon Western youth. The issue of other faiths, nonetheless, is now registered on the agenda of the Federation, albeit as a missiological problem.

Missiological Misgivings

It has been alleged that the main opposition to interrelgious dialogue at the Nairobi Assembly of the WCC came from Nordic Lutherans. In the words of a Methodist observer:

> The characteristic opinion about other world religions among Lutherans is that they are autosoteriological, spiritual do-it-yourself kits. It is not surprising that the chief attack on the Sub-Unit on Dialogue with People of Living Faiths during the Nairobi Assembly of the WCC was led by a Lutheran theologian from Norway and the theological impasse experienced at the Conference of European Churches consultation in Salzburg on "The Church and the Muslim in Europe" February 1978, was in part caused by the Lutheran block.[14]

This Lutheran opposition at Nairobi was based on the argument that dialogues and relationships with people of other faiths may be a sociological necessity and presupposed a human mutuality at the realm of creation. But dialogue at a theological level implies a religious mutuality in a way validating the truth claims of others. In other words, dialogue and conversation with people of other religious persuasions is essential for the mission of the church but that conversation is devoid of any theological significance.[15]

Following the Budapest Assembly, this point of view did generate considerable discussion in the Commission on Studies (CS), guiding the work of the newly established desk on "Church and People of Other Faiths and Ideologies." In one of the early studies of this desk, it was noted:

> Developing a suitable programmatic response in the field of other faiths has not been an easy task for the newly established office. Christians in general, and Lutherans in particular, have a varying measure of reservation and anxiety when it comes to dealing with issues of other faiths, especially on matters of interreligious dialogue. In some contexts the very word "dialogue" provokes fears of compromise, cries of syncretism, and warnings about our missionary imperative. Against this background, the LWF program has needed to proceed cautiously, taking into account the divergent contexts of the member churches and their theological sensitivities.[16]

At the first CS meeting in 1985, after the Budapest Assembly, considerable time was spent discussing such issues as the justification for avoiding the word "dialogue" in the designation of the newly established Office for Other Faiths; the rationale for maintaining a separate Office for Church and the Jewish People; the priority to be assigned for studies pertaining to "yoga," "meditation," and "Eastern Spirituality" in the West; and "dialogue as confrontation" advocated by the "Dialogue Center" in Aarhus, Denmark. The CS felt somewhat unsure of determining the direction for the work of this desk and requested that a pre-Commission seminar be organized for its benefit. In 1986, a seminar was organized in Chicago, involving Prof. Langdon Gilkey of the University of Chicago, Prof. Carl Braaten of Lutheran School of Theology at Chicago, and Prof. Ted Ludwig of Valparaiso University. The seminar included, among other things, a visit to a Mosque and discussions with an Imam. This exposure helped the CS to understand some of the issues and the theological focus of the Office on Church and People Other Faiths. The CS endorsed some of the studies that were subsequently undertaken by that Office in international, regional, and local contexts.[17]

At the international level, a "Working Group on Other Faiths" focused attention first on clarifying and allying the missiological fears about dialogue among Lutherans before proceeding to deal with other's theological issues. As the summary report stated, "a genuine sharing of witness to one's faith is consistent with respectful dialogue. In fact, it is an essential ingredient. It could even be said that there can be no genuine witness apart from dialogue. Dialogue and witness are not in conflict." Regarding the theological issues the report noted:

> An adequate theological response to religious diversity implicitly raises the question of the relation of theology to specific cultures and religions, and how this relates to the question of theological constructions generally. This situation does indeed force us to reflect on how we do theology in general, as well as on the assumptions and practices we bring to the task of articulating a theology of religion.[18]

At the Eighth Assembly in Curitiba, Brazil (1990), which focused on the theme "I Have Heard the Cry of My People," the LWF issued the most significant report to date on relations with people of other faiths. It stated:

> Since the Christian gospel is a joyful message of reconciliation, it is deeply dialogical in character and encourages us to enter into conversation with and witness to people of other faiths or no faith, boldly and confidently. Dialogue implies a two-way relationship of listening and sharing. Through dialogue, Christians attempt to carry out God's command to "love our neighbor as ourselves" as they share their experience of God's love in Jesus Christ. To engage in dialogue implies respect, concern, and hospitality toward others. Dialogue is an attitude of sensitivity, humility and openness to others. It embodies the posture of the cross in every form of our encounter with people of other faiths. Dialogue is not a disguised form of monologue.[19]

In addition to commending "dialogue as a legitimate form of ministry and witness in a religiously plural world," the Assembly report noted,

The challenge of religious pluralism leads inevitably to the need to re-evaluate and possibly [to] reformulate many traditional ways of describing and expressing our faith. As we enter the thought world of other religious communities in dialogue, our understanding of the gospel must be articulated in language, idioms, and concepts meaningful to others. This theological task possesses considerable urgency today.[20]

The report lifted up some pertinent theological issues in relation to other faiths, but also forthrightly acknowledged the "fear of the other whose faith and/or culture is different," as the source of prejudice in North Atlantic countries, and the fears of minority Christian communities in predominantly non-Christian cultures. As I have suggested so far these two issues, cultural prejudice and missiological anxiety have been the inhibiting factors in Lutheran commitment to interfaith relationships. The Curitiba statement tried to address these two issues in a positive manner:

Awareness that we Christians are one religious community among others can engender a sense of insecurity or threat. Christians should learn to look at this situation positively as an opportunity to revitalize our faith and convictions in interaction with others. Thus Christian relationships with people of other faiths today call for a careful consideration of Christian identity and vocation in the world.

The Christian commitment to witness in the midst of other religious communities is rooted in God's love for all humanity. The God we confess in our faith is not an exclusive God, but the God who reaches out in love to all nations and cultures. Our witness to people of other faiths is not only grounded in our conviction of God's universal love, but also in our deeper awareness that God is the creator of all people, the bestower of good gifts to all people, and the One who is present and works in the lives and communities of people who adhere to other faiths and religions.[21]

Curitiba thus made some basic theological affirmations, setting some directions for Lutheran relations with other faiths. By comparison, the more recent assembly in Hong Kong (1977) made no further theological advance on this issue. It is noteworthy, however, that the Hong Kong Assembly included presentations from Buddhist, Confucian, and Lutheran scholars. The theme of the Hong Kong Assembly, "In Christ—Called to Witness," motivated the Assembly to see interfaith issues primarily in a missiological framework. "We are called to witness *over against other religions*,"[22] thereby, in effect, undermining both the theological and dialogical dimensions of interreligious relations that Curitiba had highlighted earlier.

However, the address on "Justification Today" by Bishop. H. George Anderson of the ELCA surprisingly focused on our context of religious pluralism and diversity as the framework for a contemporary exposition of that doctrine.[23] Unfortunately, the Assembly report took no notice of this presentation. Nonetheless, it seems LWF has come a long way from its analysis of the "godlessness" of human environment espoused at Helsinki to, at least, a recognition of a profound religious diversity in our world at Hong Kong. Does this recognition have any ecclesiological implications?

II. *Communio* Ecclesiology and "New Ecumenism"

It is well known that right from its origins the LWF has been involved in the creation of community. The quest for Lutheran unity and communion and also the cause of wider Christian unity were born out of an awareness that the churches were being called to be agents of reconciliation, healing, and witnessing presence in the world during the first half of 20th century. Thus, the concern for the *oikumene*—in the full sense of the word, as referring to the "whole inhabited earth"—was central to the vision of the founders of both the LWF and the WCC. However, pressing problems in Europe and North America undeniably provided the necessary backdrop for discussions on ecclesiology in the early stages of the ecumenical movement.

Those of us who have pursued issues of interfaith relations are sometimes prone to ignore or forget the long and arduous path the modern ecumenical movement has taken to arrive at where we are today. Even the current self-definition of LWF as a communion of churches did not emerge out of a serious and sustained theological reflection. It evolved gradually and sometimes under painful circumstances while trying to address confessional, structural, and relational questions and anomalies in its collective life during the past fifty years.[24] Understandably, issues of other faiths played less of a role in shaping the content or the direction of ecclesiological discussions in the LWF.

While we need to celebrate what has been accomplished so far in Christian ecumenism during the last 50 years, I wonder whether this may be an opportune time to raise some larger questions for our emerging *communio* ecclesiology. I am, of course, calling attention to our present consciousness and experience of religious diversity in today's world with all its attendant problems and challenges to our self-identity at the threshold of another millenium. As we all know, the hope cherished by some Christians that the 20th century would be a "Christian Century" has turned out to be a rather naïve optimism. If anything, the 20th century, especially the latter half, ended up being profoundly diverse, religiously plural, self-consciously post-modern, and increasingly post-Christian as well. Despite all our efforts at mission and evangelism, our world, in all probability, will remain predominantly "non-Christian." Given this reality, questions pertaining to "new ecumenism" in our emerging ecclesiology may warrant greater attention than accorded to thus far. This has been voiced in ecumenical discussions for some time now. But, in some circles, raising this issue is considered as a betrayal of the ecumenical task. Others consider that issues of "new ecumenism" or "wider ecumenism" to be relevant but are not quite ready to grasp its ecclesiological significance.

Compelling arguments have often been advanced to the effect that concerns of Lutheran unity or, for that matter, of Christian ecumenism represent vastly different concerns than that of interfaith relations. Some question why the former should be a higher priority than the latter. For some Lutherans, the suggestion implies a mixing up of issues of the "two kingdoms." Others are fearful that inclusion of wider issues leads to an unnecessary "fragmentation" of the theological focus in the LWF. Furthermore, the profound conceptual, cultural, theological, or religious differences that exist among the world faiths, and a qualitatively different character of interreligious dialogues and their outcomes, if any, would suggest to some that even the very thought of "wider ecumenism" is absurd. It represents a false idealism of human unity that subverts the reconciling work of God to which the Church is called to be a witness. A collective reaffirmation of the marks of the church therefore is a prerequisite for an engagement of issues of "new ecumenism."

These are indeed weighty arguments that would counter any accusation that the emerging *koinonia* ecclesiology is nothing but a "parochial concern" or a purely "church-centered movement." That it is needs no apology. So it is important to keep in mind that those of us who raise the question of "new ecumenism" have no intention of undermining or showing a lack of appreciation for what has been accomplished in the modern ecumenical movement. The issue raised here is not one of semantics either. It is not a question of what the word "ecumenism" actually means, nor is it a matter of an "either/or"—"Christian ecumenism" or "new ecumenism." The real concern here is whether and to what extent vital theological issues that arise out of our dialogical encounter with people of other faiths have been and are taken into account in our ecclesiological reflections and in our emerging self-definition.

Put differently, interfaith issues are not merely sociological issues of good neighborly relations with adherents of other faiths in a world perpetually prone to divisions, conflicts, "cultural wars," or "clash of civilizations." Nor are these issues purely matters of a relevant "global ethic," of human solidarity, social justice, human rights, etc., about which we Christians are invariably called to act together with others.

These are not even issues of an effective mission strategy that would somehow facilitate the conversion of people from other faiths to Christian faith. Fundamentally, they are theological: they warrant a reassessment of our understanding of God, the scope of God's saving work, and of the church as an instrument of God's mission. They necessarily affect our definition of self-identity and self-sufficiency as a community in the midst of other religious communities in the world. These issues have been forced upon the churches by a new experience of our world and humankind. They are issues now widely discussed in our churches, and substantial theological reflections have emerged providing new perspectives for our theology of religions during the past twenty-five years. Strangely, our ecclesiological reflections and our ecumenical dialogues fail to take account of these developments.

Initially, concerns such as these were voiced by and among Asian and African churches in the ecumenical movement but were ignored as peripheral to the ecumenical endeavors. Today they are no longer Asian or African issues but have become issues of global concern. They have serious pastoral and practical implications for the life of local congregations, especially in North Atlantic societies that are experiencing profound cultural shifts. I am sometimes amazed at how Lutheran congregations on the East Coast of America can be so absorbed by issues in the Lutheran-Episcopal "Concordat" and their relations with Episcopal Churches across town, yet feel practically paralyzed as to how to relate to people of other faiths from Asia who virtually surround those congregations.

I want to be clear that while relationships of Lutherans with other Christian World Communions are terribly important for our self-understanding, the issue of "new ecumenism" is no less important in this regard. These are not mutually exclusive issues, as some are inclined to think, but rather they interpenetrate and shape our self-understanding. While the lifting of 16th century mutual anathemas between Lutherans and Roman Catholics may be long overdue (although the Pope thinks otherwise!), it is equally important to review critically Lutheran condemnations of the "Muhammadens" in the *Confessio Augustana*[25] and their implications for Christian-Muslim relations today. The latter is certainly a matter of life and death for Christians who live in the midst of an Islamic culture or who are intimately related to their Muslim neighbors. Issues pertaining to our relations with the majority of humankind, therefore, are no small matter and can neither be set aside nor put on hold until our churches are able to overcome divisions and differences, legacies of a different era or culture.

Perhaps a way forward is to include interfaith issues in our bilateral and multilateral ecumenical dialogues as a way of defining and testing our vision of "communio" and what it means in Christian praxis in relation to people of other faiths. For example, how we understand the classical dictum, *extra ecclesiam nulla salus* or *extra Christum nulla salus* in Lutheran and ecumenical ecclesiologies may throw more light on convergences and divergences in our doctrines of creation, redemption, justification, church, Holy Spirit, sacraments, and so on, which may provide new insights and resources for our engagement in the world of religious plurality.

This plea is belatedly, and somewhat reluctantly, noted in the recent LWF discussions on communion. For instance, the Klingenthal Consultation organized by the Ecumenical Institute in Strasbourg on *Lutheran Ecumenism on the Way* (1990) acknowledges the need to address issues of "new *oikumene*" or "new topics" in ecumenical dialogues.[26] Although this Consultation paid little attention to interreligious issues (because there was no Asian input!), it did recognize, on the one hand, the "acontextual" character of Lutheran ecumenical discussions and dialogues, and on the other hand, how context specific they were (the West and its theological tradition). There was, however, an implicit awareness at this consultation, that the overwhelmingly "textual and prepositional" orientation of Lutheran and ecumenical discussions has not only excluded real life issues facing the churches but also inhibited meaningful theological participation of churches from non-Western cultures within the Communion.

This awareness, in a sense, has opened up possibilities for a more inclusive interpretation of the concept of "communion." The concept is so elastic that, if properly understood, can include "all people" in its framework, thus broadening the scope of our ecclesiology. The most recent LWF statement published by the Department of Theology and Studies proposes this approach. The statement entitled *Church as Communion* includes sections entitled "Church as Mission" and "Communion and the Whole Humankind."[27] The concept of "communion" is here stretched to embrace the whole of humankind but unfortunately does so in a theologically unsatisfactory way.

First, the document fails to provide a proper eschatological frame of reference for communion with the whole of humankind. It will not do to state: "The church can be seen as a communion on the way to the Kingdom. Along the way, it is called and enabled to be an instrument promoting peace, reconciliation, respect for creation, and solidarity with the whole of humankind. . ."[28] This sentence implies that people of other faiths or no faith have no place or standing in the church's pilgrimage to the Kingdom, hence there is no necessity for a meaningful theological dialogue, except some practical cooperation necessary for peaceful coexistence. It is in this sense that the document contains one perfunctory sentence that explicitly refers to people of other faiths: "The encounter and dialogue with people of other faiths is a significant contribution to this process" i.e. to the process of "respect and cooperation between different ethnic and cultural groups."[29] One wonders, is that all that the Department of Theology and Studies could acknowledge after nearly 15 years of studies and publications on other faiths?

Secondly, the premise of a "Christological universalism" has been used in the document as a basis for an extended or inclusive interpretation of communion. But the statement fails to take into account the limitations and problems of such a premise seriously contested by people of other faiths. Without offering a carefully nuanced Christology such a premise unfortunately serves to reinforce a modernist or colonial vision of mission, service, and human unity.

Thirdly, this suspicion is confirmed in the following sentence: "Through mission, the communion of the church and churches is related to the world as a sign of God's creative, transforming and *final intention* for humanity and creation."[30] I am rather puzzled, or even startled, by this statement. It appears to me to be rather presumptuous and triumphalistic. I am afraid claiming that the communion of churches and its mission is God's "final intention" for humanity and creation represents not only a dubious theology but also a dangerous ideology.

Given these serious deficiencies, the document's claim that "the church as communion stretches to all people" when it engages in worship, witness, and service, becomes a cliche and suggests a stubborn refusal to address serious theological questions raised in such engagements in the world. As a consequence, this document understands worship, witness and service of a communion in the world *functionally* rather than *contextually,* which would enable the church to enrich its life, to redefine its tradition and determine its identity. Lacking a broader focus on the unity of human family in the perspective of the kingdom of God, our engagement in worship, witness and service may lose its eschatological frame of reference and turn out to be mere functions of a church-centered communion.

In conclusion, the call for a "new ecumenism" is not about stretching our concept of communion so as to make it horizontally more inclusive. It is fundamentally a call to discern the new reality facing all our churches in a religiously and culturally pluralistic world. It is a call to recognize that people of other faiths are not pedestrian bystanders waiting to be roped in through our mission or succored to in their helpless situation through our service while we march towards the Kingdom as a communion. They also claim to be fellow pilgrims, bearing the same image of God and yet possessing a different vision of God or of the ultimate goal of life, of human salvation or liberation and the meaning/destiny of human community and creation. We can, of course, choose to bypass them or to ignore their claims and religious experiences, or we can choose to engage them theologically and practically in our quest for a meaningful communion with them as we collectively journey towards the Kingdom. An ecclesiology that lacks proper discernment of today's issues and context runs the risk of becoming a theological abstraction and irrelevant. The adequacy and relevancy of an ecclesiology lies, I believe, in its ability to relate to or address concerns of Christian faith both internally and externally.[31] To take seriously the challenge of "new ecumenism" might help us overcome a posture of self-sufficiency, indifference and closed particularity evident in our *communio* ecclesiology.

Communion and the Holy Land

Mitri Raheb

This topic is so broad that one could say almost anything and yet nothing. I am sure that each of you has different expectations, which is why it was not easy for me to decide on the angle to choose for addressing the issue.

One angle would be to form the word "Communion" as it relates to the LWF's constitution, which was adopted in Curtiba 1990 and according to which the LWF henceforth defines itself as a "communion of churches which confess the Triune God, agree in the proclamation of the word of God, and are united in pulpit and altar fellowship." From this angle, I will explore the role of the LWF in the Holy Land in the past and present, and possibly in its future involvement. The role of the LWF in the Holy Land cannot be underestimated: The Diaconia to the Palestinian refugees and the establishment of a Lutheran church and communion between the different "mission congregations," may be the two most important achievements of the LWF there. To highlight this role of the LWF in Palestine would be interesting, but not exactly enough, which is why I decided to deal with the concept of communion from a different perspective. I will try to show that communion can function as the hermeneutical key in understanding what is going on in the Holy Land today, both in society in general as well as in the Christian community.

Communion as a Theological Concept

For this reason I will be using the word "communion" in a broader sense, starting with the concept of the Trinitarian God, in whose image humans are created. Divine relationality leads to an understanding of the human being as a relational being. Being human is nothing but being in relation, in relation with God and in relation with the "neighbor." Being in communion is what it means to be human. Being in communion has to do with communication and leads to the building of a community. In that sense, the church as communion is a sign of a healed community.

The fall, on the other hand is, nothing but a rebellion against this communion; it is the desire to relate to oneself only. Martin Luther describes the sinful human being as "der in sich verkriechende Mensch" (the human curved in upon self), who is living in separation, in division, i.e. in Apartheid, the result of which is fragmentation and animosity.

Communion and the conflict of the Holy Land

There are various ways to describe the context in the Holy Land: as a conflict between two national movements, or as a religiously motivated conflict. I will try to relate it to the above-mentioned theological anthropology. The conflict in and over the Holy Land results from a lack of communication, from miscommunication, and from the fear of being in communion with the "other." In the last hundred years, Jews and Palestinians have been very hesitant and fearful to relate to each other pretending that the other does not exist and that it is not necessary to communicate. This can be seen on several levels: political, economic, religious, and cultural.

Politically, the Zionist movement from its inception until recently wanted to believe the Holy Land to be "a Land without a people for a people without a Land." Throughout the decades Zionists have ignored the existence of the Palestinian Arabs in the Holy Land, as if they simply were not there. The Zionists wanted to believe that the Holy Land was theirs alone and that they didn't need to relate to their neighbors, the Palestinians. And when they discovered that they could not continue to ignore the existence of the Palestinians, they developed a policy of conquering as much land as possible, confiscating as much land as possible, and isolating the Palestinians in small Bantustans that were surrounded with Israeli settlements, and left the Palestinians no place to breathe. Then they created the so-called "bypass roads", roads that were built on Palestinian land and to be used only by the Jewish settlers, to avoid relating to the Palestinians. The outcome is an apartheid system; the goal is to prevent any communication between the two peoples.

The Arab world, on the other hand, has tried to ignore the existence of the State of Israel—to act as if it was not there. There were only few attempts to relate to this state. No communication was possible. Relating to the other (the state of Israel or the PLO) was seen as a crime. Only after the Oslo Accords in 1993, was a channel of communication between both parties was established. This peace accord simplified the necessity to relate to the other; the future of the Holy Land cannot be but in a certain kind of a communion between both peoples. With Netanyahu and now Sharon, I am afraid that we are back to square one, as recent events have tragically proven.

Economically, the conflict in the Holy Land has ceased to be part of the former East-West conflict and is already transformed into a North-South conflict. Israel is becoming increasingly part of the so-called "First World," while Palestine is becoming more and more a typical "Third World" country. The gap between them is growing every day. We now have already two totally different infrastructures, two different economies, and two different income scales. This economic separation will make any future communion between the two more difficult. Israel believes that it can survive by itself in a Jewish Super-Ghetto, and it continues to control the Palestinian economy by strengthening its dependency on the Israeli economy. A vision for a communion with the neighbor around the corner is almost non-existent.

Religiously, most of the movements within the three monotheistic religions are afraid to communicate with one another and the secular communities. Increasingly, the religious movements are becoming aggressive towards the other, believing that being religious means being separate from the other. The notion of the Holy Land is used to a greater extent in a religious, exclusive way. For a long time nationalism has been the motor behind the exclusive claim of one group to the land. Today we see that this claim is given more of a religious connotation. What is difficult to package nationalistically is marketed in the name of religion. Religion is replacing nationalism in that it gives the people in the Middle East a sense of identity in isolation from the others. The claim of being in communion with God leads to the avoidance of any communion with others. In the land where the great communication between God and the human took place, communication between the peoples of the land is missing.

The conflict in the Holy Land is becoming more of a **cultural** conflict; it is not any more a mere conflict between the Israelis and the Palestinians, but rather a cultural conflict within both communities. In that sense, it is a conflict within Israel and within Palestine, a conflict over who they are and who they want to be; a conflict between contradictory understandings of ones identity in relation to the other. People want to "have" their own identity, forgetting that their identity is established by relating and interacting with others. In the Holy Land, we are still struggling with the old question of "who is my neighbor?" For many people here, the neighbor becomes an enemy if he or she is not from the same "culture" and "ideology." The group separates itself from that. Communion is practiced only within the same group. People might live next to each other, but in reality they do not know anything about their neighbors. Ghettos are created for the different groups. Psychological barriers, concrete walls, and religious fences go up to avoid any possible communication with the neighbor. In this context, the neighbor does indeed become an enemy. Alienation becomes unavoidable. The other is seen only as a threat, only as part of a collective entity. The other does not have a face or a name. A good example of this thinking is found in Deutronomistic Theology, e.g., Joshua, Dtr. 7.

What role then can the church as communion play in such a context?

The Church as Communion and the Holy Land Today

Having described the context of the Holy Land as a context of miscommunication and of fragmentation, it is tempting to offer the church as an example of what communion ought to be. I am afraid it is not that easy. The church cannot be the solution/model for society. The process of fragmentation and miscommunication affects Christians like others. We have to be very humble when it comes to the question of a possible Christian role. We are called to repentance. In many cases we have not been instruments of healing, and often times we have not been a sign of the communion to others.

And yet, we are called by God to be instruments of reconciliation, to help break down barriers which prevent the knowledge of that renewed community among human beings, and to bring healing. In that sense, the church is not the solution for a broken community, but a sign of what communion means.

a. Christianity is a fragmented phenomenon in the Holy Land. Although Christians are a minority of 3 percent only, over 39 different denominations co-exist in Jerusalem. Each of them belongs to a certain communion of churches; a communion beyond one's own confessional boundaries, however, is seldom. This diversity is a curse and a blessing at the same time. It is a curse because it weakens the Christian witness in a non-Christian world. It's a blessing because it prevents us from ideologies that propagate uniformity as a basis for identity and community. A renewed community in the perspective of the Gospel allows for different identities to flourish, drawing them into conversation with each other.

b. There is a tension between the local Palestinian churches and their respective international partners (including LWF) present in Jerusalem because each international Christian community wants to have a foot in the Holy Land. Although there is a spiritual communion between the local church and its international partner, a real sharing of resources is still far from being reached. Often there is a certain kind of dependency of the local on the international. The situation has not changed much since the time of the apostle Paul. There was a time when the call for independence was strong in the local churches. This phenomenon was part of a larger movement of independence of "Third World" countries from the colonial powers. But both concepts, that of dependence and that of independence are inadequate for the communion between the local and international partners. What is needed today is creating of models of interdependency, a sharing and managing of the different resources within the one communion. Charity is not an answer anymore. Theological concepts alone are not of great value. Empowering each other and acting responsibly are what is needed from a communion in a more globalized world. In a context where the international community is involved in "managing the conflict," the links of interdependency between the local church and its international partners can become a possible vehicle for change.

c. The Holy Land can be the place, *per se*, for a real communion between Christians worldwide. Tourism can become a vehicle for this communion.

During the last weeks, I did a study on tourism to the Holy Land. The outcome was eye-opening for me and is, I believe, relevant to our vision for "Communion and the Holy Land."

Out of the two million tourists who visit the Holy Land every year, about. 85 percent are Christians. About 15 percent are Lutherans, which means that over 200,000 Lutherans visit the Holy Land every year. The majority of them come from Germany, the Nordic countries, and the U.S.A.

If we examine the way a Christian tour to the Holy Land is usually arranged, we find that it is organized. It usually starts with a pastor announcing the trip as a pilgrimage to the Holy Land or Israel. Palestine is not mentioned. That side of the country is avoided. Palestine is also avoided in the tour. The most important cities mentioned in the Bible are on the West Bank. Nobody visits them. Tours do not visit Hebron, a very important city in relation to the Bible because of Abraham and David. The whole of Samaria, such as Shekhem, Sabastia, and other areas are also not included. The so-called Judean desert is avoided. So many places that play an important role in the Old and New Testament are not part of the program, because these tours are Israeli-designed and marketed with an exclusive political philosophy. Only half of the Christian pilgrims visit Bethlehem, and then only for about one and a half hours. The bus drives to Manger Square; the group lines up at the church of the Nativity to see the "sweet Italian Jesus Doll laying in the Manger;" and then goes back to the bus, leaving behind nothing but polluted air.

The fact that most of the tourists, including Lutherans, bypass the West Bank reminds me of one of the most beautiful and most meaningful stories in the Bible, the story of Jesus and the Samaritan woman. When a Jewish man or woman wanted to travel from Jerusalem to Galilee at the time of Jesus, he or she would not go straight through Samaria, but would first travel to Jordan, then head upwards, and finally cross over the river again, to avoid Samaria. The same thing happens today in tourism; but Jesus refused to take part in what I would call "apartheid system pilgrimage." The Bible says that he went through Samaria intentionally. He did not have problems in dealing with the "not so pure" Samaritans. He went through Samaria, and there had one of the most wonderful rendezvous: He met the Samaritan woman at the well and had the longest dialogue ever with anyone. By not visiting Palestine, Christian pilgrims are missing exactly this encounter. What if Christian pilgrims start breaking down the walls of separation in the Holy Land?

For many of the tourists, the Holy Land functions like a fifth Gospel. They come to visit where Jesus actually lived in order to understand his life, words, and work more fully. Usually, pilgrims run the sites that Jesus used to walk. By doing this, they miss what I would call the sixth Gospel, the communion with living stones. Running through ancient ruins and sites in the Holy Land reminds me of another story in the Bible. It is the story of the resurrection of Christ. Two women came to look for Christ behind the stone, and an angel appeared to them and asked them why they were looking for the living among the dead? "He is not here!" He is not in the ruins! He is not in the ancient buildings! He is risen, which means that he is to be found among his people. Whenever they have Communion, he is there. And so, it seems to me that these pilgrimages are not taking the resurrection of Christ seriously because they are still looking for the living among the dead, and he is not there—he has risen! Imagine if only 50 percent of all Lutherans visiting the Holy Land were to experience communion with their fellow brothers and sisters. How powerful a communion could we be?

Communion cannot be a mere spiritual celebration, nor can it be a mere theological statement without any commitment. In a world of economic disparity, our Communion leads to responsible sharing of resources. When we talk about pilgrimages, we are dealing with what I think is one of the most serious economical problems of the Holy Land. If we examine where the pilgrims spend their money, we find that they spend 95 percent of their money in Jewish hotels, restaurants, travel agencies, etc. In 1995, the total revenue of tourism to the Holy Land was $278.4 billion, constituting over 35 percent of exports of services and 11 percent of total exports (goods and services). The total revenue into the Palestinian economy amounted to $151 million, constituting only 5 percent of the total Israeli revenues. Tourism actually helps widen the gap within the Holy Land between the north and the south, between Israel and Palestine. At the same time, many Christian pilgrims visiting the Holy Land want to teach us how to be peacemakers. They visit the Holy Land with a vision to do something for peace and for justice because they are good-hearted people. They do not realize that through their one-sided pilgrimage, they contribute to an economical polarization of the Holy Land and are thus now seeds of injustice. Here we have a crucial role to play as a communion.

d. Interfaith in communion: The Holy Land is the cradle of the three monotheistic religions. Many of the Christian communions are engaged in interfaith dialogue. My feeling is that the interfaith dialogue done by most of the international Christian bodies does not take the concept of communion seriously. Interfaith dialogue is often not done in communion. For example, in the majority of the international Christian bodies Christian Jewish dialogue is still shaped by a western Anglo-Saxon agenda and methodology. It is a very academic, theoretical, white middle-class dialogue. This dialogue came with certain presumptions based on European experience and European history where Jews were a persecuted minority and where Christian theologies were instrumental in this persecution. The hermeneutical key for most of these Christian Jewish dialogues was the Holocaust. In this dialogue, Jews had a monopoly over suffering, their fate as former victims of western Christian history was omnipresent. The other reality, that of an empowered state of Israel, the occupation of the Palestinian land, and the suffering of the Palestinian people was seldom an issue in this dialogue. Although Palestinian Christians are part and parcel of all international Christian world bodies, their voice was marginalized, and their experience neglected. It was not a dialogue of the communion, but of a certain segment of that communion, that took the freedom to speak for the whole communion. Most of the Jewish partners in this dialogue were not representative of the Jewish faith in general, but only of that in Europe or the USA. Western Christian theologians created a Judaism according to their own image, to suit their feelings and concepts. Because of this, Christian-Jewish dialogue was seen as categorically and qualitatively different from a Christian-Muslim dialogue, a presumption based again on a clearly western perspective, where Islam used to be a foreign religion, not much related to Christianity. The fact that Islam is part of the Judeo-Christian *Wirkungsgeschichte* (historical reality) was not taken seriously, and the communion was not realized in these dialogues. By not doing that we missed a lot of opportunities. Often a mono-cultural dialogue was exercised. The importance of a communion for this dialogue was not seen clearly. In a dialogue we need each other's perspective in both confirming and critiquing our respective concepts. Let me add one other example: It is not possible to have Christian-Jewish dialogue on the issue of "land" by bringing some Old Testament scholars together with some Rabbis. Rather, we need to hear the stories of and be in communion with Native Americans, South Africans, and Aboriginies in Australia, etc. Their perspectives on the land is constitutive for our dialogue. This is a method we are trying to develop in our Dar al-Kalima Academy in Bethlehe, "Contextual theology from a cross-cultural perspective."

e. Communing with the enemy: Transforming the enemy into a neighbor becomes the ultimate goal of a communion. Healing communal relations, establishing communication between enemies, and creating human bridges of understanding on the grassroots level is essential for our call as a communion in the Holy Land. We cannot live just by and for ourselves. At least this is not our calling. Calling is to reach out to the whole suffering community and to bless its wounds as the good Samaritan (Lukr 10:25-37). "For what shall it profit a man, if he shall gain the whole world, and lose" his neighbor? Communion is the possibility to move beyond the concept of "winning the war" into "winning the enemy," that is, to transform him/her into a potential neighbor. We have to confess that people who cannot think of reconciling even with their enemies will soon start hating themselves, and that people who are not courageous enough to cross boundaries to meet the other will soon find themselves prisoners in their own constructed ghettos, and that those who cannot do mercy to their opponents will wake up one day to see their own house collapsing over them.

The conflict is affecting the peoples of the Land. There have been always more than one people in the Holy Land. Now there are at least two: Palestinian & Israeli. They will continue to be there for the centuries to come. It is impossible for either of them to have a monopoly over the whole land. The land has to be shared, with two peoples in two independent yet inter-related states. The vision for peace in the Holy Land cannot be that of Babel: one people with one language (Genesis 11:1-9). But it has to be that of a shared Jerusalem at Pentecost: where Jews and Arabs are viewed as equals and are enabled by the spirit to communicate with and understand each other; a city open to accommodate the adherents of all three monotheistic religions as well as guests of all nations (Acts 2:1-18). This biblical vision that became a reality at Pentecost is the ultimate symbol of Communion in the Holy Land. This communion is not the fruit of our work. But it is a gift of the Holy Spirit, which helps us to communicate with each other. It is the Spirit who transforms the land of confusion into the land of communion, a land that is holy and whole.

A Response to Mitri Raheb

F. V. Greifenhagen

Mitri Raheb is a voice not often clearly heard, especially among Christians in North America. His is a voice of a "Palestinian Christian," How can that be? Palestinians are Arabs, and as my students and many in the western world assume, all Arabs are Muslims, just as they assume that all Muslims are Arabs. Raheb's voice is a desperately needed corrective to these stereotypes.

He formulates a theological framework of "communion" in the broader sense of divine and therefore also human relationality, meaning that, as humans, we are divinely meant to be in communion with each other. This "communion" means not a monologue but a dialogue, and if a true dialogue, it means addressing difference and similarity, contention as well as unity. I propose to apply and to extend this framework to three problematics that emerge from your remarks:

- the problem of our (western Christian) view of the Bible
- the problem of our (western Christian) view of history
- the problem of our (western Christian) view of the Holy Land

In each case, I wish to raise the question of whether our view is monologic or of the true dialogic nature of "communion."

Our View of the Bible

This first problem is alluded to in Raheb's passing reference to the deuteronomistic theology that justifies the erasure of the "other." In other publications, such as *I am a Palestinian Christian*,[1] he deals with this problem more explicitly. The central issue here is that, in the *Wirkungsgeschichte* of the Bible, western Christians read the Bible monologically, as a single voice unconditionally authorizing the giving of Palestine to the state of Israel, which negates the rights of any Palestinians (read "Canaanites") who are thus displaced. Politically, such a monologic reading results in the justification of a form of apartheid and of the eventual erasure of Palestinians.

A dialogic reading of the Bible, issuing out of the framework of "communion," would suggest that the situation is otherwise. For instance, Norman Habel, in his excellent book *The Land is Mine: Six Biblical Land Ideologies*, argues that the Bible contains not one but at least six different views on the land of Palestine.[2] One of these views is what Habel calls "Land as Host Country: An Immigrant Ideology" and is found in the narratives of Abraham, Isaac, and Jacob. From this particular biblical perspective, the land of Palestine is not the possession of one divinely favored group, but is a resource that is to be shared between the indigenous population and immigrant groups. While the relevance of this perspective to the present situation in Palestine as a corrective to dominant Christian assumptions is clear, Habel's work warns more generally against reading a monologic perspective on the Palestinian situation into the Bible. The Bible itself presents us with the dialogic situation of "communion," a dialogue between different perspectives and ideologies that are often in contention with one another. In this sense, it is more accurate to speak of the Bible as being both for *and* against us, as a text that is part of the dialogue, rather than to use exegetical sleight-of-hand to produce a monologic reading which, upon further analysis, tends to agree with the dominant assumptions of our social, political, and economic context.

Our View of History

From a monologic western perspective, history tends to be viewed as a progressive series of winners displacing losers, or, in modern economic terms, as a series of "hostile takeovers" (economic mystification has strongly infiltrated the sense of history in the west). For instance, Canadian history can be viewed simplistically as a series in which native control was replaced by French control, which, in turn, was replaced by English control. In each of these transitions, the winners totally displace the losers. Similarly, the history of Palestine can be portrayed as a series in which Canaanites were displaced by Israelites, who were displaced by Assyrians and Babylonians, who were displaced by Persians, who were displaced by Greeks, who were displaced by Romans, who were displaced by Christians, who were displaced by Muslims, who were displaced by Israelis. And to the winner go the spoils! Thus the complexity of the past is erased.

John Ralston Saul, a Canadian social critic, challenges such a monologic view of history with a dialogic perspective that views history as the "layering of civilization."[3] Applied to the Canadian situation, Saul argues that the English victory in establishing hegemony over Canada did not and does not result in the erasure of the native and French layers of Canada's history, no matter how much the "victors" may wish or believe such to be true; rather, the present day Canadian reality consists of a unique and complex "layering" of all these civilizational strata. Attempts to ignore or to simplify this complex layering only results in aggravating tensions. The same argument could be applied to the Palestinian situation: the present Israeli hegemony does not erase the layers of Palestinian civilization; rather, the present reality of Palestine is a unique and complex "layering" of civilizations, a complex inheritance of all that went before. Such a complex layering must not be ignored but must be acknowledged and attended to and celebrated, if tensions are to be worked with constructively.

The Christian temptation to erase Palestinians and the complex layering of civilization in the Holy Land simply in order to erase the guilt of Christian complicity in the Holocaust must be resisted as a deceptive and dishonest repetition. A truly dialogic approach for Christians will mean taking ownership of Christianity's painful heritage of complicity and then forging ahead in full recognition of the complexity of history, towards a more just future.

Our View of the Holy Land

The typical western Christian view of the Holy Land is rather romantic and is based on a simplistic and literal reading of the Bible. Thus, when Christians go to visit the Holy Land, they go to encounter the romantic image that they have already constructed. In other words, they go to Palestine to visit a museum of the idealized past, a museum in which living realities such as Palestinians (including Palestinian Christians) are either totally invisible or are typecast as "Samaritans" or other biblical villains. When I lived and worked in Israel, I would often encounter Christian tour groups at various holy sites; it was immediately apparent that these Christian pilgrims were someplace else. They were not observing the present realities of Palestine; rather, their glazed eyes were focused on an idealized or even mythical landscape populated by biblical characters. Theirs was a monologue within their own previously constructed worldview; there was no true dialogue and communion between this worldview and the world actually out there in Palestine.

From a dialogic perspective of "communion," Christian visitors or pilgrims to the Holy Land must acknowledge not only the *dead stones* of the various biblical and Christian monuments, but also the *living stones* of the Palestinians, especially the Palestinian Christians who stand in direct continuity with the earliest Christian communities. Thus, your remarks on tourism especially strike home. Rather than fostering a Christian tourism or pilgrimage to the Holy Land that focuses on an idealized past and ignores present realities, thereby playing into a monologic view that supports political apartheid and the extermination of Palestinian communities, including Christian ones, Christians need to foster an alternative form of tourism or pilgrimage which combines visits to the monuments of the past with encounters of the present.

What to Do?

So what are Christians to do? It seems to me that in response to the concerns of Palestinian Christians, as so finely articulated by Mitri Raheb, at least the following four avenues of action can be suggested:

(1) <u>Education</u>: Christians must learn to be aware that the way in which they speak of biblical Israel today has contemporary impact. Our approaches to and our views of the Bible can support and justify policies that cut and cause people to bleed and die, just as they can also support and justify policies that bring life.

(2) <u>Advocacy</u>: Christians are called to engage in advocacy on behalf of their Palestinian brothers and sisters, to clear up media stereotypes, to promote dialogue between different parties, and to appeal to their various governments to make their aid to Israel conditional on the observance of fundamental human rights.[4]

(3) <u>Alternative Tourism</u>: Christians need to foster a form of pilgrimage to the Holy Land that includes not only visits to the past but also living dialogue ("communion") with Palestinians, both Christian and Muslim, and also with Israeli Jews.

(4) <u>Becoming Learners</u>: Finally, Christians in North America and Europe need to vacate their seats of privilege and assumed superior learning and sit at the feet of their Palestinian brothers and sisters, who truly live in the intersection of past and present, of Muslim, Christian and Jew, and of overlapping cultures and civilizations, that they may learn what it means to be truly cross-cultural.

Communion within Ecomonic Disparity

Molefe Tsele

"The time for silence has passed and the time to speak has come."

Martin Luther, "To the Christian Nobility"

The 'Have-alls' and 'the Have-nothings'

The 1998 United Nations Development Programmé (UNDP) *Human Development Report* on Consumption and Human Development tells a stark story of inequality unparalleled in recent memory, certainly the worst case so far. The traditional classification of the 'haves' and the 'have-nots' no longer truly reflects the reality. What we have now are the 'have-all' and the 'have-nothing.' Try this for the latest trivia:

- The world's 225 richest individuals are estimated to have a combined wealth of more than the annual earnings of 47 percent of the entire world's population (2.5 billion people).

- The three richest people in the world have assets that exceed the combined GDP of the 48 least developed economies; over 90 percent of them are in Sub-Saharan Africa.

- The average African household consumes 20 percent less today than it did 25 years ago.

- The most affluent 20 percent account for 86 percent of total consumption expenditure, while the poorest 20 percent account for only 1.3 percent.

An even more disturbing note in this sad saga is that the disparities are set to continue. Twenty-five years ago, the richest 20 percent had 30 times the income of the poorest 20 percent—today they have 82 percent as much income.

The question is, where are these ultra-rich persons? The biggest share is in the U.S. with 60, followed by Germany with 22, and third is Japan. Only two out of the richest 225 are from sub-Saharan Africa (white South Africa, for example).

The inequalities are not geographical but also intra-regional, and within a country, there are further gender and rural-urban disparities. Consider the Case of the Two Germanys:

> In the united Germany economic activity is faced at the moment with a special challenge. In principle it is a case of the same tasks that confront economic activity in general at the present time and that are connected with such key words as compatibility with creation, social compatibility and democratic compatibility. But in the present German context the widely diverging living conditions in West and East Germany constitute a special challenge and therefore have to be given special attention.[1]

The German Evangelical Churches' Document concludes that "overcoming the blatant inequalities between East and west has become the overriding social challenge of Federal Democratic Republic"[2] and calls for a rethinking of the global economic system:

> It has become crystal clear at the present time because of various crises which have arisen that the dominant aims and value conceptions are endangering civilization's sustainability. Especially the ecological crisis has advanced the insight that a profound rethinking is called for with regard to the economic use of the earth on which we live. . .The rethinking must embrace the whole range of particular points, and are connected with the economy, its achievements and successes.[3]

It is the thesis of this paper that the levels of economic disparity as they currently exist will ultimately undermine the very notion of social cohesion. This issue poses a challenge in the first instance to social peace and stability, but even more fundamental, to any notion of community that we still have at this stage. In a word, we cannot honestly talk of our common Father while existing in such two diverse worlds of the 'have-alls' and the 'have nothings.'

It seems necessary to formulate our starting point for any Church-talk, and by implication any God-talk, from the perspective of this single biggest threat to society: the acute levels of inequalities. Indeed, it is no longer possible to talk of Americans, Germans, or Japanese, etc,. or of any notion of common citizenship. It is even more impossible to talk of communion as people of God, as those called together, or those sharing a common baptism, as those who are equal guests to the common table. The very idea of Holy Communion has become a fiction both in its symbolic and material sense in the same way that it is increasingly becoming a modern-day fiction to talk of a British nation or of any nationhood for that matter.

Thirty years ago, Latin American theologians following Medellín reminded us that, for theologians faced daily with the challenges of survival against the onslaught of poverty, the God-question does not come first and foremost from the challenge of non-belief, but from being confronted with the condition of non-person—i.e. those whom the prevailing social order does not acknowledge as persons.[4] The Latin American theological question was formulated thus: How are we to talk of God in the face of the suffering of the innocent? In the same way, it is our claim that the Church-question does not need to be posed from "purity of doctrine" but sociologically with respect to socio-economic systems and structures that hinder the possibility of authentic communion. How are we to speak of the communion in the face of the stark economic disparities between the few rich and the many poor? The new threat to ecclesiological unity does not come from theological or even ideological disagreements. To the contrary, there exists a higher degree of consensus both amongst the left-wing and right-wing theological traditions than ever in the past few decades. The challenge of our time comes from the non-community that exists across the church and within denominational families. We cannot evade the rich/poor divide any longer, more so because it becomes increasingly menacing and erodes every sense of community we have been able to nurture thus far. This may sound like a rhetorical question to you, but how can we be brothers and sisters, co-heirs, in this context? This is the problem of communion within economic disparities, which we shall seek to address in the following.

The Continuing Struggle: Economic Justice

While we cannot justly claim that economic injustices are a recent phenomenon, there is evidence that they have gained ascendancy over other issues that have dominated modern history. There can be some justice in the claim that most of our wars so far were fought for ideals such as "the fatherland," "democracy," or "freedom," etc. It can be argued that modern day wars are about economic justice. In fact, as early as the rebellions unleashed by the Reformation, the demand for economic justice was central to the pursuit for freedom. The Revolt of the Peasants of Swabia as articulated in their Twelve Articles clearly bears testimony to the claim that as early as the beginnings of the Reformation, those who were non-persons in that context refused to limit the boundaries of that freedom to a mere individual and subjective freedom of faith. While Luther will be remembered for his unsympathetic response to the demands of the peasants, it is conveniently forgotten that in his "Admonition to Peace" addressed to both the German princess and the peasants, he passed the verdict in favor of the peasants:

> These protests are right and just, for rulers are not appointed to exploit their subjects for their own profit and advantage, but to be concerned about the welfare of their subjects.[5]

Further he had this to say:

> People cannot tolerate it any longer if their rulers set confiscatory tax rates and tax them out of their very skins.[6]

It is often overlooked that Luther agreed with the peasants on almost every claim they had insofar as it was a protest against their economic exploitation. What he vehemently and almost ruthlessly disagreed with was their "mechanical theology," which seemed to say that by simply becoming "Lutheran," one would gain material benefits. Here Luther sensed the narrow wedge of a dangerous theology of self-interest. For Luther, this was simply a distortion of his theology of the freedom of believers, which to him could not be separated from a dialectical servanthood to all. But beyond that, he read a false understanding of the freedom of the Gospel, which as he puts it, is nothing else but *"Suffering. Suffering. Cross. Cross."* [7] . Luther could not reconcile the attitude of the peasants and their claims for "worldly freedom" (meaning a denial of servant-hood) with the core meaning of the Gospel of the Cross, which by definition involves willingness to suffer (we may even say the inevitability of suffering) in the service of the neighbor. Thus for him, the entire rebellion had nothing to do with the essence of being Christian. As he bluntly rebuked the peasants:

> You do not want to endure evil and suffering, but rather want to be free and to experience only goodness and justice. [8]

It is crucial to hear Luther speaking to this issue in our times partly because we risk the same temptation of opting for theologies that promise happiness and prosperity. To a very large extent, Western Christendom has capitulated to this very notion of instrumental Christianity, which promises comfort and prosperity. For Luther, being a Christian, which he took to be not as "commonplace" as many would assume but a "rare-bird," essentially means discipleship or, to be precise, a community of cross bearing and cross-bearers. A particularly troubling feature of the Christianity of our time is that it has become worse than the false religiosity of the peasants, which Luther so harshly opposed. We have inherited a theology that not only legitimates the current economic relations, but that is also dependent on them. Such is the poverty of our theology that it has been assimilated to the European culture and to a hedonist ideology of happiness and prosperity. A serious correction would have to come from a retrieval of the Biblical tradition that espoused the path of humility, endurance, and servant-hood. This comes as a gift in the encounter with those who are victims of the global economic order, those who have been rendered redundant, sacrificial victims of our civilization, the non-persons who have no worth in our calculations of Gross National Products.

Comprehending the True Meaning of the Spirit of our Time

Douglas John Hall observes, and rightly so in our view, that reality is best comprehended as it is experienced by those who are victims rather than those who mete out injustice. As he argues for the epistemological significance of the poor, the poor:

> . . . are important to the community of belief not only because they are those in and though whom the Christ is concretely with us... but also because without them we shall almost certainly fail to understand what time it is...i.e. the spirit of the time *(Zeitgeist)*.[9]

Our time has been described as an era of increasing globalization or post-modernity. In our view, the spirit of our time is the disintegration of the local, the indigenous, the national, and the communion. The enhanced ability to empathize with the tragedy one sees on television millions of miles away also blunts the ability to genuinely be in communion with one's neighbor, or even be involved with the local. We are just beginning to comprehend the full theological impact of this globalizing phenomenon. To seek refuge in 'denial' or 'behaving as if' is a sure recipe for failure. The starting point for comprehending this new *Zeitgeist* (spirit of the time) and for responding to it in ways that can result in its saving grace, is to seek to understand it not as advertised by the salespersons of the richest 20 percent, but as experienced by those groaning under its crushing impact, i.e. the poorest 20 percent of the world. When viewed from the devastation that it visits

upon the poorest peoples of the South, globalization represents a new and cruder form of colonization, which tears
apart every sense of community and indigenous identity. The
arrival of McDonald's at the remote corner of the village may
be seen as the entry onto the global highway, but the ironic
impact of that new era is that very soon, the national cur-
rency, the indigenous cultures, and the local peoples ways of
surviving will die a slow but certain terminal death. The
condition of entering the new club of global players is the
willingness to take ones place at the bottom-end of the heap.
In our view, that is the issue, that determines the Kairos for
the Church and which can only be fully comprehended from
the growing economic disparities that currently define global
relations. We are convinced that the extent of the problem
requires a heavy corrective dose of theological dogma and
praxis. Hall was partly speaking to this situation when he
called for confessional theology to take precedence over
professional theology. As he says, unless the Church exposes
itself to what is endangering the life of its world *"it will be
incapable of confessing the faith. It will be imprisoned in the
professional mode."*[10]

From Professional to Confessional Theology

The Reformation ushered in an era of passionate
confessionalism. It was no longer sufficient simply to believe.
One had to be precise about beliefs and about that which
such confession excluded. In the history of the Church, such
confessionalism has not been common, and it has only become prominent during those times when the Church felt its
proclamations at stake. The precision and appropriateness of
the Church's proclamations for a given era separate the confessional church from a merely professional church. At the
height of the apartheid struggle in South Africa, the tradition
of resistance or struggle tradition within the church identified
this particular stand of the church as a prophetic stand, that is
an attempt by the church to speak directly, uncompromisingly
and appropriately to the spirit of the time. Theology in a
confessing mode means that the church speaks in a way,

which addresses the human situation and reality authentically. The Kairos Document observed that the Church is in the habit of conducting its theology either as captive to the powers of the day (state theology) or in an abstract and metaphysical way, and addresses imagined and superstitious fears in a timeless warp. In its prophetic mode, Confessional theology refuses to proclaim reconciliation where the word of judgement is appropriate and condemnation where grace would be fitting. Confessional theology is a living theology of a believing community. It is held passionately, even to the point of martyrdom.

> *What is required of a truly confessional theology is not only that it should participate in the struggles of its context but that it should do so without the comfort of ready-made solutions.*[11]

It is not casual, indifferent, or whatever happens to be in fashion. Confessional faith implies suffering and passion. It is precisely, then, when we avoid this suffering that many resort to being professional theologians. Confession signifies discipleship. In this context, we need to ask as the stepchildren of confessional theology of the Reformation: What word does our Church have for the 20 percent poorest of the world? How does our theology assist the church to be awakened to the spirit of the time and to fulfil its given responsibility for this era, especially the church of the richest 20 percent? As Luther warned, "the time for silence is has passed and the time to speak has come." What is our message? Are we in agreement that what the church is busy with hardly speaks to the millions of the debt-ridden poor of the Third World who do not understand how they came to be indebted without showing anything for such debt? What word do we have for the economic order that has gone off course, to put it mildly? How do we remind it of its true calling, namely that economies are God's instituted orders to enhance life, to contain evil excesses, and to protect the poor and vulnerable? How do we recall the biblical jubilee tradition, which reminds us that economies cannot be autonomous masters accountable only to themselves or guided solely by the profit motive but that they must function within limits defined by the inner good for people and for the environment? How do we particularly protest the deadly gap that continues to grow between the 'have-alls' and 'have-nothings'?

Reviving the Tradition of a Community of Confession

Most of us have the misfortune of being introduced to important theologians by way of second and third parties. And as it true with every story, once it is retold over several sources, it tends to take shades and versions slightly different from the original, and at times, even go to the extreme case of becoming the opposite of the original story. One such theologian who has suffered that same fate at the hands of fellow theological travelers is the famous Latin American liberation theologian Gustavo Gutiérrez. A little known aspect of his theology of liberation is his concept of liberation, which he argues, finds its full meaning only in the meaning of communion with God. Where that communion exists, there liberation finds expression. For Gutiérrez, liberation has three reciprocally interpenetrating level of meanings, namely, the socio-economic level, the personal human level, and finally, communion with God. Thus communion with God gives meaning to the essence of the sacrament called church. In and through this form, unity and communion find expression. The mission of the Church is to bind together, to provide the basis for fellowship and unity. As he says:

> To proclaim the Gospel is to call human beings together as a church , to announce the mystery of filiation and fellowship. . . a mystery hidden for generations now revealed in Christ.[12]

Within Gutierrez' concept of liberation, communion with the self, with others and ultimately with God is fundamental. Where genuine fellowship is lacking, their sin and alienation prevails; therefore there is no liberation. We can find here an important component to our reconstruction of communion within economic disparities. Essentially, these divisions do not only separate us from one another (social alienation) but they also separate us from communion with God.

Being a Displaced Church in Solidarity with the Poor

It is not enough to simply identify the church as the mystery of fellowship with God. In reality, the church takes particular institutional forms in history. While this fact has to be seen within the inner mission of the church, which is to bring all persons into fellowship, questions have to be asked about the nature and place of the church in history—more precisely, where should our church be located if it is to be a confessing community? Luther has always been critical of the church that finds its place in imperial courts rather than in seats of humility. Perhaps the best confessional theologian to remind the church of its place in the present history was Dietrich Bonhoeffer, for whom the prior ecclesiastical question is not the how or what of the church, but the where—i.e. the question of the place of the Church during Nazi Germany. For Bonhoeffer, the place of the church has to be determined by its displacedness. The church is in the world, more precisely, in the secular arena, at the privileged places of the world, within the establishment. For Bonhoeffer, this place of the church is a sign of the disobedience of a church that is unwilling to be in the places where Christ is present. That question is also still relevant for us and for the crucial question we are considering. In an era such as ours, is it relevant to ask the whereabouts of the church? Is the church with the super-rich 20 percent or is it where the poorest 20 percent are? Then again, is the church everywhere, as professional theology would want us to believe? The question for us is not simply where is the church, but where is the Christ of the Church? We must warn that this question should not be answered in a static manner, as if the Christ has chosen to pitch a tent and make His dwelling amongst one group against the other. When he was invited to do that in the Gospel story of Transfiguration, he resisted the temptation and chose to descend to the valley where His ministry was needed. The answer to the presence of Christ of the Church is, therefore, answered by his ministry. The church is where Christ is active, defending the innocent, liberating the oppressed, giving sight to the blind, and creating community where there is alienation and meaninglessness. The church is present where struggles for life are taking place, where resistance to evil is taking shape, where the gospel of liberation is being proclaimed, where the confessional faith of the humility of the cross is being proclaimed, where the works of love are done. This is the contextual answer to the question of the place of the Church. But we cannot leave the impression that the Church is universally present with the same richness and vigor everywhere. The church is particularly present where it is being humiliated and crucified.

Servanthood as a Form of Being in Communion

It is difficult to talk of the humiliation or servant-hood of the Church in the era of Christendom. In Africa, where Christianity dominates, one commonly hears complaints when Islam is given equal status to Christianity. Many of us are accustomed to being the establishment church, and we have lost sense of what it means not to count. Given the economic marginalization of 47 percent of the world's population (the world's poor), many of whom, especially in Africa, are Christians, we feel threatened. In the context of the spirit of our time, characterized as we argued above, by gross economic discrepancies, is it perhaps not appropriate to ask the question of the church, not so much from its place of triumph and glory, but from its humiliation and suffering? Douglas J. Hall, in an essay on the future of the church, asked whether is it not better to accept the "churches' belittlement" as a way of having faith in its future? It seems to us that the church's way to contend with the present challenge is to adopt the model of servant-hood. There is no possible way of addressing the current gaping divide except by way of taking the model of the community of the cross, marked by self-denial, sharing, and servant-hood. The route of guilt and counteraccusation would only serve to further condemn both the poor and affluent. The Gospel is not simply a soothing message to comfort the guilt of the rich, but presents them with the opportunity to participate joyfully with the present Christ in combating the structures that resulted in the present shameful divisions between the super-rich and the poorest of the poor. As a confessing communion that seeks God's guidance to follow Christ's example and to be co-workers with Him in the work for justice and life; we can do that, and can only do that with the full assurance that it is God's work in the first instance and that we are privileged to partake in it. There should be no illusion, however, about the discomfort that such work will bring. To begin with, the very poor whom we are committing ourselves to serve, may return our service with scorn and contempt. Secondly, there are no assurances that we have lasting solutions or ready-made answers to this endemic problem. One necessary element of being a servant church is to adopt a posture of openness to others, and to serve in humility. That is what it means to be a humiliated church. We hold firm to the belief that it is in the path of the humiliation of the cross that the church will be an authentic communion in a world that welcomes grave disparities. That is how we, the Lutheran Communion, born of a confessional faith of struggle, can make our contribution to the present world, a mold deeply in the crisis of its own making, the urge to be richer, bigger, and number one.

Response to Molefe Tsele

Karen L. Bloomquist

Dr. Molefe Tsele has so powerfully laid out an agenda for us. I will resist the temptation of picking away at aspects of his presentation, and instead plunge more deeply and concretely into the implications of a communion theology. I do so by asking what does this mean concretely for us as North Americans?

To move quickly to the central point: we in North America (especially the U.S.) face a situation of competing gods. The global economy functions like a competing god for us, with its pervasive effects and assumptions—the primacy of self-interest, insatiable wants, competition, unlimited economic growth, and profitability for a few at the expense of the vast majority.

These are only some aspects of the credo of a free market "religion" that has been and continues to shape or re-create the world in its image, demanding ever-greater sacrifices from those with so little to begin with. In other words, a deeply theological or confessional issue is raised for Christians, embedded as we are in this global economy.

How then does communion move us toward addressing more effectively the economic disparities that Tsele has so clearly pointed to? How might a deeper living out of communion move us beyond the usual guilt-filled, hand-wringing paralysis that so typifies the reaction of those who live amid the economic power centers of the North?

Living into and out of the divinely-empowered reality of communio—where we interact, stand with, see, hear, and feel what we would not otherwise—we have been brought together as the Body of Christ. We have been transformed by a reality that moves us into the hard, difficult, often controversial work for economic policies and practices that will lead toward a more "sufficient, sustainable livelihood for all." I want to suggest four examples of how *communio* might become more concrete.

(1) As I've been working on the ELCA economic life statement, I've especially been influenceded by some of my students at Wartburg Theological Seminary—from such places as Tanzania and El Salvador. At the LWF *communio* consultation in Tanzania last August, I suggested that one implication of *communio* is that Christians of the South would hold us in the North accountable for challenging and seeking changes in how policies of international financial institutions severely impact people living in the South. The Jubilee/2000 Campaign to alleviate the debt of severely impoverished countries, in which the ELCA actively participates, is an important example of doing just that. Interestingly, one of the Tanzanian bishops immediately responded that in turn the North should hold churches in the South accountable for challenging corruption in their governments that keep any debt relief from benefiting the people.

(2) ELCA "companion synod" relationships between synods in the North and the South have led to increasingly deep relationships and mutual benefits. Yes, important material benefits flow to the South through these relationships, but these are small compared to the potential transformation of societies that could occur on the basis of these relationships. What about the places of responsibilities in which members of these North American synods live out their ministries in daily life? How might the economic decision-making they carry out there affect people in the developing world and bring about larger structural and policy changes for the sake of all?

(3) *Communio* also implies holding ecclesial institutions, such as the Lutheran School of Theology at Chicago (LSTC), accountable for engaging the pantheon of free-market thinking, whose most influential center is located at the University of Chicago. What would it mean for LSTC faculty and students to engage with those there who are shaping the global economy? If we're facing a situation of competing 'gods' or

faiths, wouldn't this itself be a form of inter-religious dialogue?

(4) Taking *communio* seriously also suggests how we might better face and deal with tensions within the Lutheran communion here in North America, such as the relationship between congregations in poor and affluent areas. Or how might this affect how we view and address the farm crisis? The situation in North America reached such desperate straits that farmers in Montana—many of them part of the Lutheran communion—demonstrated against and tried to blockade hundreds of Canadian grain trucks as they come over the border. The trucked in grain depresses even more U.S. grain prices, which is likely to lead to a huge percentage of farmers losing their farms and their livelihoods. How do we as United States and Canadian Lutherans deal with that ethical dilemma in light of communion?

These are just a few of the difficult economic challenges we face today. No easy or simplistic answers will suffice. It is tempting to give in to cyncism, fatalism, and a sense of the inevitability of economic disparities.

But instead, we have been grasped and shaped by a power that becomes real for us in the Body of Christ, through the communion of saints. The communio is a power that sustains and encourages and keeps us "hanging in there" amid the hard challenges of seeking to rein in the free-wheeling, often devastating power of the global economy. And it is through these tough, tenacious kinds of engagements that we might discover anew the heart of what we confess.

Communities of Women and the Lutheran Communion

Monica J. Melanchthon

Introduction

The commemoration of the 50th anniversary of the Lutheran World Federation leads us to look back and recall our history. Also it is a time to celebrate joyfully and to soberly take stock of ourselves at the beginning of the twenty-first century. Our inheritance is rich in faith and works as we have been reminded. It nourishes us for the tasks of today and tomorrow. This is also a time to reflect and to catch a vision of ministry and service that is worthy of our past that builds upon our present and thrusts us again into the mainstream of human life with the message of God's redeeming love. This is also an opportunity for us to reestablish our identity and our purpose through the discussion of our identity as a Lutheran communion, and to articulate what we wish to accomplish and how we will pursue our goals in the years ahead.

I would like to explore with you one very significant and urgent issue: the role and status of women within the Lutheran Communion. It is exciting not only to reflect on the varied and often controversial currents that swirl around women's daily lives, struggles, and victories in the world today and within the Church, but also to look at the challenges that lie ahead.

My proposals are tentative. I simply want to reflect upon the information gathered in light of my own experiences and background, and you will supplement it with your own experiences and insights.

As roughly half the world's population, women would hardly seem to need to struggle for attention. Yet struggle is precisely what they have been doing during these last decades of the 20th century. Their endeavors deserve no less a word than revolution—in expectations, and in accomplishments, in self-realization and in relationships with men. It is a revolution which, though far from complete, promises over time to bring about changes as profound for men and women as any that have occurred in the recent past.

The challenges that women face in the world today are manifold and highly complex. First, the issues that confront us are multi-layered and take place on multiple levels: economic, political, social, cultural, and religious. They occur in the private and public spheres; they include issues of race, caste, class, gender, economic security, and sexual orientation. Second, the issues are entrenched in systems, structures, cultures, family values and have very deep historical roots. They involve many actors and perpetrators, the powers and principalities in our societies, the men and women in our lives, and even our very own selves. Third, they are expansive and pervasive, highly globalized and tightly interconnected. In addressing these challenges, feminism does not, therefore, speak with only one voice. There are many voices with different stories and sometimes contradictory messages. A universal woman does not exist; hence the need to speak of "communities of women" who assert and fulfill their needs, aspirations, and desires through different feminisms. To accept the differences among women as a part of our starting point means that we will have to be critical of the other as well as critical of the self. This will relativize the universalizing attempts of women who hold dominance in terms of class, caste, race, sexual orientation, or education.[1] A special effort is needed to listen to these feminist voices—voices pleading, or protesting, aggressive, angry or shrill, voices wise, strong, and resourceful, voices that carry power and call for a response.

What is it That Women Want?

A long time ago, I once read a quote that said, "If you think that equality is the goal. . .your standards are too low." I thought of this as I began writing this paper. Often the question, "What do women want?" is given the answer "equality." Are we clear on the meaning of this term? Are we all agreed that this is the answer? Most often, equality is understood as fair access to the necessities of life, often articulated as "equal pay for equal work."[2] Women who can prove to be "like men" are rewarded, while those who choose to be homemakers get nothing because their work does not count. Ina Praetorius correctly says:

> In the prevailing order, the question of equality or difference can initially amount only to whether women submit to the 'superior' which offers itself as a criterion for equality, or whether they accept the place among the others, the 'inferiors,' which has long been assigned to them.[2]

The attempt to achieve such "equality" has enabled many women to enter into arenas traditionally not welcoming of women. In medicine, law, and business management women's participation has increased. Women lawyers have spearheaded reforms in the treatment of female victims of rape and of battering. Women executives have created supportive networks to help other women up the ladder and strive to sensitize corporations to the special needs of women, such as flexible hours, maternity benefits, child care, and parental leave. Women journalists have fought to get women's concerns on the front page. Yet, overall, little has changed. Has the presence of women in these "nontraditional" occupations influenced the culture to be more sensitive to the needs of the marginalized, or has it changed the ethical standards of business or management? I am not questioning the validity of the claim to equality, but want to remind us of women's long experience of prejudice and the consequent feminist claim of empathy with the victims, the oppressed, and the marginalized of either sex. Has women's way of doing things changed the manner in which institutions are run?

So, why have women not made more of a mark? It may be too soon to expect vast transformations. For one thing, women in elite, fast track positions are still pathetically scarce. We need to remind ourselves of the idealistic vision that helped inspire feminism in the first place. The women's movement, like other movements of oppressed groups, carries with it a critical perspective that has been forged in the painful experience of rejection and marginalization. When that perspective is lost or forgotten a movement stands in danger of degenerating into a scramble for personal advancement. While we need to celebrate those who "have made it," so to speak, we need to be cognizant of the fact that the majority of women are still far outside the gates of privilege, waiting for the movement to begin again. This female majority is still seeking ways to survive uncaring institutions, exploitative work places and the deep social inequities, which remain unchallenged by the few who have attained success in those arenas.

Equality with men is a fine ambition, but ultimately, assimilation with the dominant is not good enough. If such is the understanding of equality, and that is our goal, our standards are too low. So, what is it that women want? Women do not seek to exchange places with men. Women want better places in a kinder, gentler, less rigidly gendered world. The special heritage of values and priorities that traditionally have been associated with women as wives and mothers are sources of strength, able to create an enlarged vision of society. A society so enlarged and strengthened and transformed will make more room for everyone's dreams.

The following two illustrations may help clarify the issue. The first is a poem written by an anonymous Indian dalit woman who writes about her hunger for food—a reality that characterizes millions of people in the world.

Every noon at twelve

In the blazing heat
God comes to me
In the form of
Two hundred grams of gruel
I know him in every grain
I taste him in every lick
I commune with Him as I gulp
For He keeps me alive, with
Two hundred grams of gruel.
   I wait till next noon
And now know he'd come:
I can hope to live one day more
For you made God come to me as
Two hundred grams of gruel.
   I now know that God loves me—
Not until you made it possible.
Now I know what you're speaking about
For God so loves this world
That He gives His beloved Son
Every noon through You.[4]

The second example is a story I heard at a workshop. A Chinese woman worker, who, during the time of modernization and economic restructuring in China, was retrenched from her job as a worker in a factory. To earn her keep she had to travel two hours on her bicycle to work as a baby sitter for four hours. For her labor she was paid a salary of 24 Yuan or US $3. When interviewed by a reporter about the "Women Go Home" campaign in China, she simply said, "If I want to buy myself a hairpin, I will have to ask my husband. I cannot bear to see the look on his face!"

Pardon me for only giving Asian examples, but this is the area where I live and work and where, as a result, I have seen the conditions described above. I could give other examples, but I think the glimpses of these realities are enough, enough not only to portray what is real, but also to present the challenges and the questions they pose. For both the poem and the story speak of a reality and a desire that cannot be addressed or repressed by such grand narratives as gender equality or national strengthening or modernity. Rather, they remind us of what is really at the heart of the dreams, struggles, and hopes of the majority of women in the world in the past and also today.

Now that some women have a foot in the door, it is perhaps time to pause and to figure out what we will do once we get inside. Equality with men may be a fine ambition, but ultimately assimilation with the dominant is not good enough. If such is the understanding of equality, and if that be our goal, our standards are definitely too low. So, what is it that women want? Women do not seek to exchange places with men; women want better places, better places in a kinder, gentler, less rigidly gendered world. The special heritage of values and priorities that have been traditionally associated with women as wives and mothers are sources of strength able to create a broader vision of society. A society so enlarged and strengthened and transformed will make room for every person's dreams.

The Challenge of Globalization and Women

In a recent article Jerome Binde, the director of the Analysis and Forecasting Office, UNESCO, identifies four pressing issues that threaten the survival of humankind as it lurches toward the new millennium. They are growing inequality, maintaining sustainable development, finding global solutions to global problems, and finding and maintaining peace.[5] He concludes by saying:

> Globalization cannot be confined to the worldwide expansion of telecommunications, computers, the mediasphere, and markets.

> It must be founded on greater international democracy and on anticipatory conception of democracy, the main pillars of which are: a new social contract for the

21st century; sustainable development, that is to say a "natural contract"; a new international contract encouraging world-wide regulation and integration; a culture of peace and ethics for the future; and life-long education for all.

More than anything else, "globalization" is becoming the defining word of this era in all manners of discourse and in all manner of context. But what does it actually mean? At its most basic,

it can refer to a multi-dimensional phenomenon of global relationships and global inter-dependence, a complex set of linkages between societies in social, economic, political, and cultural spheres. This set of linkages, however is neither equal nor beneficial to all who participate or are forced to participate.[6]

"Globalization" is fraught with adverse consequences, particularly for the less powerful: a loss of sovereignty; a widening of marginalization; an increase in poverty and growing unemployment; a degradation of the environment, and an expansion of violence and repression with a proliferation of national, ethnic, and religious chauvinism.

The meaning of "globalization" goes beyond its definition as a concept, its aspect as a process, or its nature as a phenomenon. We need to consider "globalization" because it has a direct bearing on the people we seek to serve: the poor and vulnerable and marginalized. We need to see and understand at the economic, political, social, and cultural level, for example, how global power relations affect women, migrant workers, the unemployed, the media and even health care.

While greater international interdependence undoubtedly contributed in some measure to world-economic growth in the early post-war period, it also created vulnerability. Greater international interdependence meant increased subordination of national economic development and national sovereignty to international considerations that were driven by the interests of the most powerful players. Specific events in the past two decades have shown the inherent fragility and instability of a world-political economy oriented at corporate and profit seeking interests. This combined with the consequences of unequal international economic relations helps to maintain gender inequality.

Under the new world economic order, or globalization, global economic liberalization has had and continues to have profound implications for women, for their work and their life chances, depending on their country's position in the global economy. While the shift to export-oriented strategies made more jobs available to women, thereby creating a specific female industrial labor force, the conditions of employment and the characteristics of this type of industrialization have also sharpened gender inequalities.

Women's specific position in the economy is determined where economic programs, the role of the state in these programs, and the reality of women's subordinate position in society intersect. Gender inequality across countries and societies allows men privileged access to the scarce and valued resources of society, including wages, employment, leisure, health care, education, personal autonomy, and decision-making. Women's subordination results in segregation – denial of access to certain jobs or lack of access to higher positions. Women hold secondary positions in the economy, uniformly receive lower wages than men, carry double burdens for paid market work and unpaid reproductive work. Lower levels of education, a lack of control over their own sexuality, and a lack of formal political power characterize the majority of women. Gender inequities in the allocation of resources, in access to social and economic opportunities, and in the distribution of social services translate into inequities of income and in control over income and health. Indeed, in the drastic and rapid restructuring of economies in globalization, women pay the heaviest price.

Key economic programs have had a negative impact on women. The emphasis on an export-oriented industrialization as a growth strategy pursued now by newly industrialized Economies are killing the agricultural economy on which many of the people hitherto depended on. These have also brought large numbers of women into the manufacturing labor force, sharpened gender inequalities, and has led to the re-creation of disadvantages, the exploitation of women's sexuality in the factory site, etc. It has also led to social and personal changes, disruption of family life, and multiplication of women's burdens as women's work in the Trans-National Corporations and export manufacturing subordinated women more directly to a global market.

Structural Adjustment Programs (SAPs) which were imposed on countries with huge balance of payments deficits and which prescribed austerity measures, import liberalization, and cut downs on state subsidies to health, education, and other social services. In periods of structural adjustments, malnutrition and infant mortality rates have risen, as did proportions of high-risk pregnancies and babies with very low birth rates. We continue to witness the deadly consequences of SAPs. Like India for example, where the statistics about women and children are most revealing. Fifty-three percent of India's children under age four are underweight and malnourished. Eighty-eight percent of all pregnant women between ages 15-29 suffer from anemia and are malnourished. Six hundred forty million Indians have to do without basic sanitation. Two hundred ninety-one million adults are still illiterate and every year there are 2.2 million infant deaths.

The recent past has seen an increase in military violence, especially sexual violence; labor migration; continuing, emergent and resurgent issues of identity—ethnic and national; self determination and sovereignty; religious fundamentalism; and in general the violation of human rights.

At the heart of economic globalization is therefore a paradigm of development, which is based on reductionism, fragmentation, homogenization, and commoditization of nature and human beings. This paradigm runs contrary to the laws governing the nurturing and reproduction of life in ecosystems. The ecological crisis, which the project of development has spawned, "suggests the indispensability of nature and the impossibility of substituting its life-support processes."[7] The response to this crisis by genetic engineering, supported of course by multi-nationals, is that nature is dispensable because Science can find a way of replacing or multiplying it. With this, life becomes a new commodity and the "distinction between science and the market blurs."[8]

Some of the most pressing issues that women are addressing include increased poverty (70 percent of 1.3 billion poor people in the world are women), economic exploitation and threat to survival, the unabated international trafficking of women and exploitation of women's sexuality, intensified violence, and ecological issues.

Women's movements today are dedicating themselves to struggling for and creating/building societies where women are not only equal to men, but also where those women, children, and men are empowered to live full human lives. This struggle entails transforming structures, institutions, relationships, and values not only in the broad spheres of economics, politics, and culture, but also, and just as importantly at the level of inter-personal relationships, family, and community life and individual selves. This includes our self-understanding and identity, self-empowerment, and development and our sexuality. The responses involve advocacy efforts in issue based initiatives, rallying against forces that have kept us poor and powerless, developing alternative development paradigms and strategies that are empowering, sustainable, and gender sensitive and to ensure that feminist perspectives impact on the various facets and questions of development. Women's movements have grown stronger, gained space, assumed confidence and clarity, and are able to take on more issues and are able now to influence and impact public opinion. This has contributed to the increasing ability to take on collectively and publicly, issues which traditional culture and religion have found difficult to do, for example: marriage, divorce, reproductive rights, and sexuality.

Greater impact and influence has also meant the co-optation of women and gender concerns by governments and other forces that use the rhetoric and pursue token reforms but are in most cases for the preservation of the status quo.

Women and the Church

By and large societies have been ahead of the churches in recognizing women's rights as full human beings. Women were excluded from participation in leadership, ministry, and ordination because of the Church's casting of the nature of God and of the human being in generically male terms. But with the recent access of women to higher education and theological study, women have been able to challenge the patterns of male dominance in both social and ecclesial contexts. There have been many women who have and continue to function as catalysts for change, as prophetic voices, and as healing agents in a hurting society because of their love for Jesus Christ. They continue to listen to the Voice who says,

> Get you up to a high mountain,
> O Woman, herald of good tidings;
> Lift up your voice with strength,
> O Woman, herald of good tidings
> Lift it up, fear not;
> Say to the cities of Judah,
> "Behold your God." (Isa 40:9)[9]

While many of the churches have accepted the feminist critique of the Christian tradition and admitted women into ministry, there are still several churches that continue to be hesitant or rather closed on the issue. This stands in contradiction to the assertion of equality in creation (Gen 1:27), and in Christ (Gal 3:27-28), and indicates a deep incoherence in Christian theology. Women continue to challenge this discrepancy and seek to be recognized as equals in terms of being qualified to minister to fellow Christians within the Church.

Women are also conscious of the fact, that they are also members of a larger society and therefore any discussion on "wholeness" or "community" should be extended beyond the confines of the Church to include the larger struggle for the wholeness of humanity. This involves recognizing and responding to the cries for liberation from widespread oppression that is casteist, classist, or racist, oppression in which people of other faiths are caught up as well.

A more essential reason for exploring a communion of men and women in the churches is to grow into a renewed, redeemed, and redeeming community within the global context of desperate struggle against exploitation and poverty, violence, hopelessness, and despair. In simple words, the struggles of women within the church cannot be addressed without taking into consideration the larger struggle for integral human liberation as promised by God. Addressing and responding to this is part and parcel of the church's prophetic and caring ministry.

Women and the Lutheran Communion

Men and women are made in the image of God and are equally included in the salvific plan of God. All believers are equally redeemed and therefore equally eligible to serve and this forms the basis for any philosophy of Christian life and service. God makes no distinction based on race, class, caste, or gender. The Jew is no more or less redeemed than the Gentile. The rich person is not more or less redeemed than the economically disadvantaged. The westerner is neither more or less redeemed than the citizen of the Third world. The woman does not have a new-birth process that is different from the man. All believers are made new and are called to be servants of Christ to be in right relationship with God and with one another.

What then is the task of the Lutheran Communion? Is there in fact anything we can do or say that could be of consequence, and if so who will do it or say it?

Within the Lutheran churches, much has been achieved through the dedication and work of many individuals and the Women's desk of the LWF. I would like to call your attention to two documents written very recently which highlight the many achievements in relation to women within the Communion. The first is an article entitled, "Communities of Gender and the Communion of the Church," written by Dr. Musumbi Kanyoro.[10] The second is the evaluative report on the LWF/DMD Desk for Women in Church and Society 1988-1997, entitled "The Unfolding Vision," which outlines the Federation's commitment to the empowerment of women and the work and achievements of WICAS over the last ten years. In the following few paragraphs I share some tentative reflections on the subject.

I. Feminist Theory and the Church: The problems confronting women today are global in nature. These problems cannot be approached as separate problems or experiences for different groups of women or as matters of objective study. We need to focus on the relationships among these issues and among those most affected by them. Hence, we cannot look only at female sexuality without paying attention to AIDS. We cannot study domestic violence only but also the global violence against women as refugees and victims of war. I see the immediate task of the communion as one of addressing the manner in which the global economy works and how women can find a place in it from which they can support themselves and their families. I would like to emphasize the

> need for church and society to engage in extensive dialogue with women's analyses of social theory. Such dialogue is necessary in order to discover and utilize the new insights emerging from the experiences that women bring to shape a social theory upon which the church's ethics are built.[11]

II. Transformation of Values and Attitudes: The LWF's commitment to the empowerment of women has certainly produced very concrete and positive results, and this work needs to continue and be strengthened. Partnership between women and men as a constitutive element of our vision is relatively new. If it is to become a reality, then we must be intentional in finding the appropriate channels and strategies to address the issue at all levels of the Federation's activity – local, national, regional and global. I do not see the problem as being a structural one anymore. I think we have enough mechanisms instituted to ensure the participation of women. But we need to confront our deepest values with regard to sexism within the society and the church. Our task is to work towards the transformation of values and this needs to be at the core of our engagements especially in our leadership formation programs, in the actions we take to address ecological issues and in our commitment to women's empowerment and men-women partnership.

This is easier said than done. While there are men who have a certain commitment in principle to women's liberation, their own life styles are often rather traditional. They project expectations derived from their interaction with mothers, sisters, and wives on the women leaders in the Communion who have broken away from traditional patterns of behavior. I therefore see a continuing need for the presence of WICAS, which not only represents the voice of women in the organizational structure of the Communion but also focuses and enables women to reflect on specific women's issues. This will ensure that women are involved as *women* and not just in a role supportive of men.

III. "Women" or "Gender"? It may be appropriate at this juncture to bring up the proposal of converting Women in Church and Society (WICAS) into Gender in Church and Society (GICAS).[12] I do agree that "gender," namely the meaning attached to sex differences is a more adequate category than "women." This is so because "gender' enables social and cultural differences to be taken into account, enabling us to move away from biological determinism.

Sandra Harding, in a recent article, outlines five aspects of "gender" which are important for us to pay attention to. First, that gender is a relationship between men and women. Second, gender is produced primarily not by individual choice but more fundamentally by social structures and their culturally distinctive meanings, created and maintained by structural and symbolic relations. Third, gender is always inextricably inter-locked with class, race, ethnicity, religion, imperialism and if I may add, caste and any other structural and symbolic system. Fourth, gender relations are dynamic and historically changing. Fifth, gender relations are always power relations—struggles over scarce resources, material or symbolic.[13] Thus strategies for improving women's situations must always address issues of power imbalance.

I may not be familiar enough with Gender Studies to assess adequately the validity of changing the name of the desk. However, I will raise some concerns. While "gender" is a more inclusive term, we will still be addressing women's issues. I do certainly agree that we need to work towards changing and transforming the attitudes of men and even women by challenging them with the gender agenda. Yet, I am a little uncomfortable with the name. I am not sure we are ready for a change in title. Women are definitely visible in terms of representation within the structures of the LWF. Yet, at the local level, there is still much to be done in promoting and making visible the participation of women. I do not see that the presence of women at the international level, in decision-making, etc., necessarily reflects the position of women at the congregational level. Work is being done to better this, but we are still far behind our goal. Until the vision, policies, and programs of the LWF are translated into reality at the local level, we need to focus on women as 'women' and their empowerment. But this needs to be done simultaneously with educating and challenging the Church to deal with the gender issue.

Furthermore, we need to be cognizant of the fact that there are many differences among women and men in the same culture. As pointed out by Harding, gender identity is not shaped by culture alone but also by the class, caste, and race of an individual, and these radically affect the experience of being male or female within a given culture or society. Gender therefore cannot be analyzed on its own without taking into consideration the linkages between caste, race, and class and how they are experienced through gender. Some more reflection needs to be given to this aspect of gender and how this might play upon the working of the Communion. Because of their special nature women have a distinctive and important contribution to make to the life of the church, and it is necessary that these unique contributions be recognized and utilized for the enrichment of life within the communion. The Lutheran churches are a communion of men and women only when they validate the God-given experience of women and make them visible at every level of their work.

IV. The need for intimacy: We live in a world where the stress is on individual rights that seem to ignore social relations. Feminist theory connects the self with others, so that individuals are not only free, but also are also active members of human communities.

One of the strengths of women is their capacity for intimacy. We need to be reminded that we are a Communion —a community of people—and that there is a subjective dimension, which needs to be addressed and nurtured. I say this because I see a wide gap between the LWF Offices in Geneva and the member churches and their congregations.

If we are to be truly a communion, there needs to be a deep personal relational pull at the center. We need to recover a capacity for intimacy with our own people and our neighbors. We need to develop a humanly vulnerable yet tight solidarity of communities of people who are deeply attached to one another, drawing warmth and sustenance from the fierce fire of commitment and love that is at the center of what binds us together.

V. Representation: We have already established that there is no uniformity in the experience of women and hence we need to be cautious and self-critical in our efforts at creating a certain version or understanding of equality. The WICAS documents celebrate the representation of women within the decision-making bodies and programs of the LWF. My question here is, who are these representatives? Whom do they represent? I say this completely aware of my own complicity as a middle class educated woman in the economic exploitation of women belonging to lower classes. I am by virtue of my education privileged to be here. I am conscious of the fact that I occupy positions of helplessness and of power in different arenas of my life.

I have in the earlier section of the paper spoken of the need to hear the voice of the marginalized. In the collaborative discourse that is happening among women in the communion, are these silent voices given a hearing? To what extent have we paid heed to the subjective experience of these women, who do not have a chance to represent themselves in discourses about women or women's participation in the life of the communion? How do we bring what is marginal to the center of our discussions? I guess this can be done only by giving the marginalized a voice, by enabling them to talk about their experiences.

Those of us conscientized and us who are privileged need to make a conscious effort not to project ourselves as the desired image, but learn rather to respond to the situation of the oppressed and marginalized sister instead of trying to speak for them, or to them. We need to develop what I have heard called a "double consciousness." This is to be conscious always of our own positions and formulations, of not using these to oppress people, but to change meaning and change the way things are by being open to the perspective of another and change mine if necessary.

VI. Regionalization: I do think that you will agree with me when I say that institutions, if they are to remain relevant to the changing times and to the needs of movements, need also to be transformed. The Federation's adoption of a regionalized structure confined the role of WICAS to performing administrative functions, as well as enabling the flow and interaction of the regions through a communications program. The work of the Federation, national, regional and global is important. The national and regional are important because ultimately, it is at these levels that the issues are most felt, that struggles are ultimately waged and won, and that alternatives are being developed. But the global is also important because all major issues in the world today are interconnected—the situation of women around the world may vary, but they result from the same "globalization of apartheid." The space at WICAS to facilitate learning, sharing of experiences, and the building of solidarity links needs to be available not only for the sake of women in the regions, but also to allow the vision of WICAS and its programs to be grounded in the dreams, realities, and struggles of the women in the grassroots. Hence, efforts need to be made to strengthen the regional offices and ensure the participation of women at the regional level. Inter-regional meetings and opportunities for sharing stories and experiences are also important.

VII. Women's Search for Meaning: As the 21st century begins, women find themselves at a critical juncture, a moment perhaps, for reflection and evaluation. The cozy limited roles of the past are still clearly remembered, sometimes fondly. The future looms with so many choices that the freedom it promises can be frightening. The massive dislocation in our cultural norms regarding marriage (even in the so called traditional societies) divorce, pre-marital sex, the roles of working women, and the definition of valued feminine attributes can be clearly heard in the stories of women. While individual women in one to one conversation may paint a fairly consistent picture of quiet coping, most are still quizzical, questioning, searching, and curious about those changing issues and their possible resolution. From my own conversations with young women, I have discovered that the overall mood toward women's issues is of searching indecision.

In light of this search for meaning, what seems to be lacking is opportunity for much dialogue. Women seem to be lonely questioners in their need to find resolution of the issues. The Church's ministry of preaching, teaching, and inquiry is seldom adequate as a source for informing their daily lives. Along with structuring ways for more sharing, the church needs to recognize changing needs and realities for women by encouraging them to take the initiative in developing educational programs that speak to current issues in their lives.

VIII. Women and Theological articulation: Women, due to their position in society, have rarely been in the forefront of ideological production and especially "religious ideological production."[14] There are still too few women theologians. It is therefore not surprising if the domain of theology has normally remained in the control of male intellectuals who, at times could have, but failed to rethink women's position. The question is to what extent women actively need to intervene in religious ideological production. Much has been said about the need for encouraging and including the feminist viewpoints into theology. I hesitate to repeat what has already been said, but will instead reiterate the need to continue listening and incorporating the voices of women in theology and their imagery which is not only an expression of their aspirations but would certainly contribute towards the transformation of patriarchal institutions and the realization of true communion. To this end, the LWF needs to continue its efforts to train and educate women through its capacity building programs.

IX. The Ordination of Women: This is still a highly controversial subject in several churches within the communion. In many churches where the ordination of women has been accepted, ordained women are still a token number, low paid, and holding marginal positions within the decision-making bodies of the church. There is still much to be done in this arena of the church's ministry.

X. How do we survive our differences? The topic of "difference" among women has been touched upon. Difference is one of the distinguishing marks of the communion— the diversity of cultures and races represented within it. This difference has to be maintained. This does not mean that one culture has the right to claim superiority. Communion and the expression of solidarity are all possible in spite of the differences that exist between the communities of women. Solidarity is not based on similarity, but on the recognition of difference. On what do we base our solidarity? Can we force solidarity across cultural barriers by appealing to our Lutheran heritage alone or do we have to look for other alignments, a certain unity, which can be used as a strategy in pushing through our agenda and experiencing communion?

In our radically polarized society, we need to construct contexts to promote dialogue, dialogue that seeks collaboration rather than dominance, that seeks common ground rather than consensus.

Conclusion

The LWF came into being against the background of material need, spiritual hunger, and in the midst of a world torn to pieces by war. Against this background, Gudrun Diestel, a German Lutheran woman, spoke of "practical needs" and the need for reconciliation.[15] I do not think that this need has been completely addressed or met by the LWF. We are still in need of reconciliation.

In conclusion, I will say that what we require is some sort of breakthrough between communities of men and women, and women and women, that continue to remain segregated. I borrow this concept from Rosemary Haughton, the British feminist theologian and author of the book *The Passionate God,* who uses "romantic love" as a paradigm for the life of Jesus and his involvement with people. In the environment of his time, Jesus himself was experienced as a physical expression of breakthrough. He was the living link between the liberation from slavery in Egypt, the prophetic critique of economic exploitation, and religious bondage on the one hand, and to the promise of the Kingdom of God on the other: a society of plenty and justice for all and of peace where everyone can take part in decision making, where lamb and lion dwell together and children play at the viper's hole, where swords are converted into ploughshares and people rest under their fig trees. He stood for healing the sick, sharing bread and fishes with the poor, setting the captives free, announcing doom to the rich who would not share, incorporating women and all sorts of other outcasts in the community.

Paul summarized this breakthrough character in his famous statement, that in Christ there is no master nor slave, no Jew nor Greek, no male nor female (Gal 3:28). This means breaking away from class, society, caste, communalism, nationalism, and patriarchy. Obviously, such a breakthrough, though perceived in a flash at a particular historical moment, can only be implemented in a long and tedious historical process of which we are still a part. But in order to be a true communion, we need to work towards the achievement of such a situation in which people can live in harmony and peace. This would be the work of love. It implies breaking away from traditional role expectations. It does not mean that this breakdown of barriers can always be lived without difficulty. In fact, separation, suffering, and dissension will be inevitable. But the breakthrough of love gives us a critical criterion and a vision of truth and what life is meant to be. Breakthrough also means that love cannot be private, confined, but that it overflows and permeates the environment, transforms others, and sets us free in a most comprehensive way.

The truthfulness of our commitment to this task has indeed to be measured by the extent to which we are prepared to fight against the systems that keep us separated. This is not just a matter of church policies (though, no doubt, to fight exploitation and patriarchy within the Church is a stupendous task). We, both women and men, have to leave behind our patriarchal values and also be able to communicate with forces and mass movements in society at large who have committed themselves to fight against capitalist exploitation and violent as well as subtle patriarchal control over women. Healing and a life of the wholeness are possible if we reach out for them in persistence, hope, and struggle.

Communion and Reconciliation

Wanda Deifelt

A presentation on a topic such as communion and reconciliation might look to some of us like one of those movies
whose end we already know after the first five minutes.
Everybody knows where it is heading and everybody knows
how it will end. That is why I plan to take a different path
and to problematize the issue a bit, maybe still arriving at a
happy ending. I would like to grapple with some of the
theological underpinnings of reconciliation and propose a
liberating model, one that is not fixed on dogmas, but on the
lives of human beings as children of God.

I want to place this reflection in the framework of communion, a notion that has been strongly emphasized in the
recent publications of the Lutheran World Federation. As
communion, the church integrates both a vertical and horizontal dimension: it is communion with God (the creator,
redeemer and sanctifier) as well as with the members of the
body that make it up: the brothers and sisters who profess the
same faith.

This notion of communion is best described in the statement *Toward a Lutheran Understanding of Communion*,
where "the church is the creature of the gospel of the Triune
God who creates, reconciles, and renews the world. By grace,
God calls us into the communion of divine life. This foundation of the church in the World of the Triune God is witnessed in the biblical proclamation of its reality as *koinonia*."[1]
There is obviously a strong Lutheran underpinning to the

affirmation that fellowship is established both between Christ and believers and among believers simultaneously.

The need for reconciliation

Within a theological setting, reconciliation is mostly described as reestablishing relationship with and reconnecting to God. Ever since the fall, humanity has betrayed God's confidence. Human beings are marked by sin, which theologians describe as disobedience to God's commands, pride, will-to-power, selfishness, or considering oneself the center of existence. Because of this tendency toward sin and evil, human beings do wrong, disrupting the relationship between themselves and God and among fellow human beings.

Thus, in traditional theology, the need for atonement is based on two basic notions. First, human beings are seen as alienated from God and incapable of transcending the immediate reality of sin and transgression. Because we are finite, we cannot restore the original reality of creation through our own efforts. Despite free will, humanity tends toward evil. Hence the second basic notion: it is necessary that God intervene. God's intervention in history is fully accomplished through the incarnation of Jesus Christ. The life, death, and resurrection of Jesus Christ translate the self-emptying of God into history and extends God's mercy and grace to humanity. Jesus Christ takes over our sins and dies on our behalf.

From a secular and humanist perspective, most people do not perceive the need for reconciliation with God. They do, however, perceive the need for reconciliation among human beings. Any newspaper article or magazine photo shows that human relations are disruptive and are characterized by much death, hatred, and pain: ethnic and religious wars; children on the streets scrambling to survive by selling crack or cocaine; sex tourism and child prostitution; unemployment; famine and disease.

The need for reconciliation among human beings requires first of all the acknowledgment that there are conflicts, diverging interests, and broken relationships. Most often we tend to overlook the conflic,t or at best, seek tolerance toward difference. Reconciliation, however, also involves naming the conflict and then working on it in order to overcome it. Within the church, the general tendency is precisely not to name conflicts, but to stress the need for a spiritual journey toward God. In truth, reconciliation with God needs to translate into and be expressed in concrete forms of reconciliation among human beings.

There are dangerous consequences to not naming conflicts but acting like false prophets who say "Peace, Peace when there is no peace," which is especially noticeable in the lives of women and children who suffer violence and sexual abuse. In the name of peace, churches have long kept silent about the terror experienced by children, by survivors of physical abuse and incest, and by women who are battered and physically violated in their own homes. In Brazil, a home is not a safe place for women. While 90 percent of the violence suffered by men takes place in the public arena (on the street, at their workplace or in bars), 90 percent of the violence suffered by women takes place within the home, and is perpetuated mainly by men within the circle of family or friends.

Reconciliation needs to be encouraged, not to maintain the status quo, but to proclaim quality of life, life in abundance. God's grace is extended to us so that we may extend it to others. In the process, we may make mistakes, but the fear of making them should not paralyze us. God demands a prophetic voice from those who are passionately committed to spreading more signs of life and hope in the midst of hatred and death.

The Brazilian novelist, João Guimarães Rosa, wrote a book about a simple, poor man who lives in the backlands of Brazil. In the midst of poverty, famine, disease, and violence this simple man, named Riobaldo, shows the wisdom that grows out of the his life experience and nevertheless is able to experience God's presence even in the midst of turmoil.

"How couldn't God exist? With God existing, everything gives us hope: a miracle is possible, problems get solved. But if God didn't exist, we would be lost in the midst of this turmoil, because life is a mess. (To live is very, very dangerous). If God exists, then we can take risks, because everything will end up well. But if God didn't exist, we would be allowed nothing at all. Then there would only be pain and death."[2]

God's reconciliation with humanity

Most theological discussion about reconciliation is based on the notion of Christ's expiatory death (Christ died for the ungodly). The Biblical basis of this concept is found primarily in Paul as he writes in Romans 5:8-10:

> But God shows his love for us in that while we were yet sinners, Christ died for us. Since, therefore, we are now justified by his blood, much more shall we be saved by him from the wrath of God. For if while we were enemies we were reconciled by the death of his Son, much more, now that we are reconciled, shall we be saved by his life!

Already in the first century, one of the most common ways of interpreting Jesus' death was based on the traditional Jewish understanding of expiation. A theology of satisfaction or atonement required a penalty or suffering to amend a wrongdoing. This understands God as judge, which Paul clearly shows in his reference to the wrath of God. Human beings are not capable of walking the straight path and keep falling into transgressions. God requires that sins and errors be corrected, and this can be done only through Jesus Christ, who takes over the sins of humanity, carries the cross, and dies in our place.

This theological construction is even more clearly stated in Paul's second letter to the Corinthians:

> All this is from God, who reconciled us to himself through Christ and has given us the ministry of reconciliation; that is, in Christ God was reconciling the world to himself, not counting their trespasses against them, and entrusting to us the message of reconciliation. So

we are ambassadors for Christ, since God is making his appeal through us; we entreat you on behalf of Christ, be reconciled to God. For our sake he made him to be sin that knew no sin, so that in him we might become the righteousness of God. (2 Corinthians 5:18-21)

The Pauline formulation, so strongly emphasized in Lutheran settings, affirms that justification can never be achieved through human works or merits. God reaches out—and out of pure grace offers his Son as a sacrifice, so that reconciliation with God can be achieved. Thus God reconciles his own judgment with the suffering and death of Jesus Christ. Still, reconciliation remains at a divine-human relationship. Hence, to be ambassadors in order to announce such reconciliation is achieved only because one who was without sin was sacrificed, and this established righteousness.

However, to take Christ's death as the absolute norm for reconciliation without considering it a consequence of his life and ministry can have dangerous consequences. Having been beaten by her husband who came home drunk, a woman went to a spiritual guide to complain and ask for advice. After listening to the woman's sad story he recommended: "Go home, put on a nice dress, and stop bickering at him. Try to make yourself pretty for him. If you are nice to him, he will be nice to you. You have to do the best that you can. Everybody has a cross to carry. This drunken husband of yours is your cross. You have to think of your children. Everybody needs to sacrifice a little. You have to think of them."

We all may agree that this is theology at its worst. But it is not a theology lacking in foundation. Its foundation is based on the notion that in order to make peace or to reconcile, somebody needs to be sacrificed. The death on the cross becomes a false model for conflict resolution: somebody needs to die in order to reestablish peace. It is a hypocritical definition of reconciliation because the conflict is not stated and worked out. It is like pushing all the dirt under the carpet, and then calling the house clean.

A clear understanding of the death and resurrection of Jesus Christ can only come if we see them as consequences of a life and ministry committed to the well-being of the poor, the outcast, the disabled, the diseased, women, and children. The affirmation of human dignity, the empowerment of those on the fringes, and the inclusion into the community of those who were considered nothing—*that* is the ministry the church needs to proclaim. That is where reconciliation starts. Death is not the purpose of reconciliation. But because this new message turns old-fashioned ideas upside down, it might become a threat. Jesus' death happened once and for all because it says: No more death. I came to bring you life, and life in abundance.

According to Paul, reconciliation can only occur through Christ. Informed by a new awareness—that of being new creatures, no longer sinful but saints—humanity can now engage in a new form of relationship that represents a new beginning. This communion, called *ecclesia*, is the body of Christ. It is cleansed of all its blemishes. In it, the baptized have had their sins washed away and are thus enabled to rehearse a social order different from what society in general dictates. "As many of you as were baptized into Christ have clothed yourselves with Christ. There is no longer Jew or Greek, there is no longer slave or free, there is no longer male or female; for all of you are one in Christ" (Galatians 3:27-28).

Reconciliation among Human Beings

Reconciliation with God implies reconciliation with other human beings, thereby presenting the ethical consequence. Luther comprehends it like this: "On the one hand we partake of Christ and all saints; on the other we permit all Christians to be partakers of us, in whatever way they and we are able."[3] When interpreting Luther, Heinrich Holze comments,

> In other words, for Luther, the *communio* between Christ and believers is inseparable from the *communio* of believers among themselves. The order is, however, not reversible: the vertical (sacramental,

confessional) *communio* comes first and is a prerequisite for the horizontal (ethical) *communio*.[4]

A broader understanding of reconciliation, one that is based upon the reconnection between creatures and creator, is presented through the notion of communion (the body of Christ).

> For in him all the fullness of God was pleased to dwell, and through him God was pleased to reconcile to himself all things, whether on earth or in heaven, by making peace through the blood of his cross. And you who once were estranged and hostile in mind, doing evil deeds, he has now reconciled in his fleshly body through death, so as to present you holy and blameless and irreproachable before him. . . (Colossians 1:19-22)

The Chinese artist Dr. He Qi, whose artwork was used for the poster of the Ninth LWF Assembly in Hong Kong, depicts this invitation to reconciliation at the table of bread and wine. Christ, with his open arms, is ready to embrace the whole of humanity. Sinners and saints are welcome. All find a place under the protective arms of the divine. However, whereas Christ is all-encompassing, human beings continue to belong each to his or her little group. Humanity continues to be divided. What is the way? Some of the people in the painting point up to heaven, some point to the side, to others, and some point to themselves. They are busy hands, hands holding a fishnet, a jar, an oil lamp, or even a bag of money. This is a picture of humanity, humanity as it is invited to make peace by the body and blood of Christ.

Reconciliation with other human beings is an outcome of the reconciliation with and by God. Overcoming disparities and dichotomies between class, race, gender, or denomination can only happen through Christ, insofar as the baptized assume their new role. The christological emphasis has the ethical imperative as a consequence. To be baptized into Christ is to put on Christ. The way to reconciliation is through the divine, since our human efforts could never lead us to overcome the social barriers that prevent communion. Of course, contemporary theologians are well aware that such reconciliation acknowledges the embodiment of the baptized, unlike some of the early church fathers who permitted the participation of the socially outcast, especially women, because women had souls and souls have no gender.

Coming back to Dr. He Qi's painting, one of the most striking features are the eyes. As I was admiring the big poster in the Assembly hall in Hong Kong, it suddenly struck me that aside from the vertical and horizontal perspective the artist was introducing a new concept: the inclined lines. Then I counted the eyes. There were fifteen eyes total, divided in three categories: Five of them point up, to heaven. Five of them point sideways, including the eyes of Christ. They look like the eyes of an equal. The other five are inclined. They are the eyes of those who look up from the bottom with humility or reverence. I found this an accurate description of the situation in which humanity finds itself. Some are only concerned with heavenly matters, and forget to look sideways to see what their brothers and sisters are doing. Others cannot look into the eyes of others because their backs are bent in humiliation and suffering. Only a few have the accepting, embracing, and life-affirming eyes of Jesus.

The Gospels offer further information on reconciliation.

> So when you are offering your gift at the altar, if you remember that your brother or sister has something against you, leave your gift there before the altar and go; first be reconciled to your brother or sister, and then come and offer your gift. (Matthew 5:23-24).

Here, the order is slightly distinct. Reconciliation with a fellow human being does not come from the reconciliation with God, but precedes it, if we are to understand the bringing of an offering as a form of atonement, or retribution, in order to promote reconciliation and set the path straight again. On the way to reconciliation to God, there is an awareness of a broken relationship with another person. Christians, then, are urged first to go and reconcile with their brothers and sisters, leaving their offering behind.

The passage goes hand in hand with Luther's affirmation about the Sacrament of Communion: "That is real fellowship, and that is the true significance of this sacrament. In this way we are changed into one another and are made into a community by love."[5] To change into one another does not mean simply to tolerate difference. It means to recognize diversity as a gift, so much so that "the other" is respected and valued. To be like the other, the stranger, the unknown, means to divest ourselves of the certainties and truths already known. When we are changed into one another we are able to experiment with and experience a different viewpoint, especially when we experience the otherness of poverty, discrimination, racism, or physical disabilities. This change can only happen through a deep sense of commitment and a wish to reestablish justice. Then the community of believers ceases to be "saints" but assumes partiality on behalf of the other. As Luther said: sin boldly—to uplift the rights and affirm the dignity of those who do not have them!

We need to recognize that although Lutheran theology gives us a strong foundation for the priesthood of all believers, our churches have not always been visible signs of reconciliation. On the contrary, we have fallen into the traps and temptations of this word, repeating within our churches the same power games, discrimination, and ostracizing that we see in any other social organization. We need to repent and ask for forgiveness for not being communities to those who are of a class, caste, race, ethnic group, or sexual preference other than what we consider normative.

When the 1990 Curitiba Assembly defined the church as communion it strongly affirmed the principle of *ecclesia semper reformanda*.

First, it is "a *spiritual* communion, **bound** together in the Holy Spirit through our common faith in God our Father and Jesus Christ;"

Second, it is "a *sacramental* communion, **called** by the gospel, **united** in one baptism and **gathered** around the same table;"

Third, it is "a *confessional*" communion, **grounded** in Scripture, the ecumenical Creeds and the Lutheran confessions;"

Fourth, it is "a *witnessing* communion, **cooperating** and **sharing** interdependently with our Lutheran sisters and brothers and with other believers;"

Fifth, it is "a *serving* communion, **bearing** the suffering and pain of others and serving as instruments of God's mercy and injustice to the world."[6]

The Curitiba Document echoes the words of Riobaldo, who presents the opinion of the common folk about religion. While orthodoxy, inter-religious dialogue, and reconciliation is still a touchy matter for representatives of church structure, it has long been practiced by the simple Brazilian people. Riobaldo says:

> What I think the most, test, and explain is: everybody is crazy. You, sir, I, we, everybody. That is why we need religion: to cease to be crazy, to get sane. Prayer is what cures from craziness. In general, that is the salvation of the soul. . . A lot of religion, sir. I myself, miss no occasion of religion. I drink water of all rivers. One alone is too little, it is not enough. . . I pray Christian, catholic, but I accept the prayers of my friend Quelemem. His doctrine is Spiritist. But when I can I go to Mindubim, where Matias is a born-again Methodist: we accuse ourselves of being sinners, we read the Bible aloud, and pray, singing their beautiful hymns. Everything quiets me down and lifts me up. Any little shade refreshes me. But is all very provisional. I wanted to pray—all the time.[7]

We constantly need to be reminded to acknowledge the goodness in other human beings and to identify the divine in them. God made humanity in God's own image. To look into the eyes of another person is to see the divine and to acknowledge the dignity in all forms of life. Prayer is a powerful way to overcome differences and to promote reconciliation through spirituality.

> 'Forgive us our trespasses, as we forgive those who trespass against us.' The effect of praying for our enemies is that we see them differently. They too live within the horizon of God's kingdom. A shift in perception fuels a shift in behavior. We treat the enemy differently, perhaps with distance, but no longer with censure.[8]

In prayer we also ask for forgiveness for not always being able to overcome differences and prejudices, and point to the Kingdom of God as the horizon of true reconciliation.

Reconciliation with the Whole creation

Humanity is also in desperate need to reconcile with creation as a whole and to ask for forgiveness in the mismanagement of natural resources and the uneven distribution of wealth. It is true that the larger portion of resources and their consumption is concentrated in the northern hemisphere. For example, the amount of electricity consumed by one U.S. citizen is equivalent to that of two Europeans and of 900 Nepalese. But we also have to recognize that the countries in the South have not paid enough attention to ecological issues. The second largest incident involving contamination by radiation in the second half of this century, after Chernobyl, happened in Brazil because of the improper disposal of an X-ray machine. It was simply dumped in the garbage, thus contaminating people, animals, rivers, and soil.

Human self-centeredness has a terrible effect on the whole of creation. We think that natural resources, land, and air are inexhaustible, and sadly, we are learning that human beings have not understood the call to be stewards of creation. Instead, we understood it as an endless source of wealth and power. This attitude needs to be corrected, and that begins with reconciliation with the whole creation.

The Church's Commitment to Reconciliation

The fragmentation and separation that characterize the structures of our society call for a more pro-active position of the churches in promoting reconciliation both at the local and the international level. Christians cannot pretend to hide under the false cover of distance from this world's affairs. Christ's incarnation is the best sign of God's love for this world. The embodied God is the real call to solidarity among human beings. In the Lutheran tradition we affirm the justification of sinners by grace alone. So we are invited to proclaim the grace of God to a world that is in deep need of solidarity and needs to overcome the division between rich and poor, north and south, east and west, male and female, white and black or indigenous. We are invited to testify that death, poverty, injustice, discrimination, and suffering will not prevail. Christ's death and resurrection says that no more suffering is needed, but that life shall abound. Let us accept the invitation to be promoters of peace and reconciliation wherever we are.

A Vision: Culling Some Prophetic Thoughts

Vítor Westhelle

The Foreword of biblical reflection calls for prophetic voices in a world in which profiteering outdoes prophesying. From the subsequent writers we see this call fulfilled. Accented voices from around the world speak intelligent, lively, image-laden but also harsh words are still resonating in our hearts and minds. In this closing chapter, I say that I'm no prophet, nor a prophet's son. I just plow some books, plant some words, and harvest some thoughts.

What we can witness by the papers of this conference is not seen simply as a closure in which we celebrate 50 years of an organization that has gathered almost all the Lutherans in the world. While the papers in this book grew out of a call to celebrate an anniversary, probably the most striking result is the fact that the laudatory voices were only a counter-point to prophetic challenges, to issues not fully addressed, to agendas that call for agents. Yet the tone is not one of whining and lamenting the failures. It is a hopeful tone, one that addresses the critical issues and does not dodge the problems, and one that identifies the crises as moments of possibilities. This conference was itself an exercise in possibilities. In fact, a model for addressing the issues was not only suggested but also practiced in the very discussions we have had. I would like here to offer but one reading of some of the challenges and issues that I consider most pressing and promising, like an artist laying the broad strokes to canvas before painting in the details. But before I do that, I would want to offer a very brief review of what I regard to be the general trend in how the role of theology in the Lutheran World Federation has developed during these last 50 years.

We can identify three periods as marked by the assemblies: the first from Lund (1947) to Helsinki (1963); the second from Helsinki to Dar-es-Salaam (1977); and the third from Dar-es-Salaam to Hong Kong (1997). We find the crucial moment in theological development in the Evian Assembly in 1970.

In the period from Lund (1947) to Helsinki (1963), we have the initial development of a crisis in theological conception. In Lund theological self-understanding was so evidently at the core of everything that theology was not even one of the five departments then created;[1] it would be created five years later in Hanover. The very metaphor used in Lund for the theological task was the all-encompassing need to rebuild the "ruined walls of Jerusalem" (99). The metaphor of wall gave expression to what the concerns really were: "Unity of faith [is] reflected in the common body of doctrine"(71). In Hanover (1952) this approach was still dominant, the image of building or rebuilding is still kept,[2] but tentative questions start to emerge as to the importance of the relation between theory and practice, between doctrine and existence (143). In Minneapolis (1957) this became structurally formulated by the recommendation of both the Commission on Theology and on Liturgy that the latter be integrated into the former. But still the dogmatic emphasis was dominant. The building of walls was the theme. And the wall was to separate doctrinally Lutheranism from secularism and from an irresponsible ecumenism (the target being the Roman Catholic Church and to a lesser extent the Reformed tradition).[3]

The crisis surfaced in Helsinki (1963) during the frustrated attempt to pass the statement on the doctrine of justification. The problem was framed in terms of two views of the human condition. A fundamental biblical and confessional anthropology that had not been questioned before was now challenged by a contextual anthropology ("circumstance" language was introduced). Without direct reference to Lund, the wall metaphor was inverted: Christ "has broken the wall of hostility," cf. Ephesians 2:14).[4] The result was the failure of the Commission on Theology to have its document on "justification" adopted by the assembly. The time when professional theologians of high reputation were able to lead and shape the theological identity of the LWF was withering.

The second period that leads us from Helsinki to Dar-es-Salaam marked a transitional stage, at the center of which is the controversial Evian Assembly in 1970. Much is known and debated about this assembly. Theology was here conceived in a new way.

Two of the then world-leading theologians present in Evian, Heinz Eduard Tödt from Germany and Gustav Wingren from Sweden, changed the nature of the theological contribution as it was known in the LWF until then. A new tone in respect to the confessional heritage was introduced. In the case of Tödt, Luther was criticized in the keynote address. The very motivating quest of his theology ("How can I find a gracious God?") was conceived within a debased monastic context by an "isolated monk" with a "deeply anxious conscience." And as such should not be "used, therefore, as the leading motif either for theology or for preaching."[5]

Wingren, in turn, took a drastic hermeneutical stance and proposed that article VII of the Augsburg Confession offers the freedom for "*more* than merely 'unity of churches'." A socio-politically informed theology was to dominate the Department of Studies in the following period, exemplified by the two-volume study on *The Identity of the Church and its Service to the Whole Human Being* published in the mid-seventies.[6] The understanding of mission as service to the world definitely turned the wall metaphor of Lund upside down.

In Dar-es-Salaam, the trend culminated in discussions on *status confessionis* in relation to apartheid in South Africa.[7] Dr. Manas Buthelezi of South Africa gave the best illustration of the new emphasis of this period. He called for new confessional barriers. "The drawing of a new confession is a matter of a redefinition of boundaries within which the unity of the church is possible" (93). These new boundaries are now to be drawn, not along traditional theological and confessinal allegiances, but along economic and political divisions in society.

The cycle was complete: the Lund motif, the wall metaphor, is repeated in Dar-es-Salaam. The role of theology once again returned to the ecclesiological discussion. But if at Lund confessional and doctrinal unity were conceived to strengthen the identity of Lutheranism, in the 1970's that identity had to be reinvented from the concrete social, economic, political, and ecclesial experiences of the churches worldwide, going even beyond the institutional churches, as Wingren had suggested. The significant critical confrontations that had to be faced in the first period—secularism and a hasty ecumenism—are now welcomed as significant positive challenges.

In the following period, up to Curitiba, the contextual concern of the theological task was brought to fruition in a department that addresses questions ranging from worship to social systems, education, women's issues, youth, ecumenism, and the encounter with other faiths and ideologies. If this array seems to suggest a theological inflation, it also represents a significant fragmentation of the theological agenda. Normative and confessional issues give way to a pluralistic conversation where voices of the Third World start to emerge with more consistency. In the first period, foundational confessional questions were dominant. In the second, the debate provoked a methodological shift and a relocation of the semantic field of the theological discourse. In the third period, starting with the predominance of an inductive methodology, the focus was again largely on substantial issues which still relate to social, political, racial, and gender issues, but focused much more on the concrete ecclesial experiences of the different churches.

In Summary

The first period was characterized by its emphasis on dogmatic unity. It defined the role of theology in terms of providing a dogmatic foundation for the unity and the mission of the Lutheran family. A look at the methodological structure of the proceedings in Lund makes this clear. By and large, the argumentation is professional and academic. It moves from principles to definitions and then to practical (missiological) applications. The spokespersons (which were actually spokesmen) for theological affirmations were mostly theological professors from Germany or Scandinavia. They brought their academic approach and credentials into the theological practice of the LWF. Theological professional competence in the tradition of established European universities was a requirement for entering into the conversation. The Luther Congress founded in 1956 gathered the theological academic resources to lend its support to the LWF theological identity and buttress the confessional walls. The subjects of the theological discourse are the "sages." The sages are those who speak the truth as foundation, the ground for what is. With a look from the outside, the sage describes what the case is and suggests the answers that will convey identity. The sage defines.

The second period is marked by prophetic denunciation. It signals the crisis of the model dominant in the first period. The crisis announced itself when still mainly European theologians were no longer able to accept a common statement even on the doctrinal core of Lutheranism: the doctrine of justification. Helsinki could be seen as a premonition of the dramatic events that would shake Europe, and hence the LWF, in the 60s. Evian (1970) is the culmination. There, the still dominant European voices joined to a certain extent by the Third Block (USA), would raise their voices denouncing injustices in the world. The last minute change of the venue of the assembly was highly emblematic. It was the North Atlantic world that from the outside raised the prophetic voice of denunciation. The prophet took the place of the sage, however, still standing outside in an alienated condition. Prophets, so went the argument, are able to discern better what is taking place inside. They are the seers in a world in which even the victims don't realize the fate that besets them.

Contrary to the sage, the prophet is not an enunciator of what is, but of what ought to be. The new definition of *status confessionis*, as it came to be discussed in Evian (1970) and defined in Dar-es-Salaam (1980), emerged exactly after no agreement on the *articulus stantis aut cadentis* (the article by which the church stands or falls) had been reached in Helsinki (1963). The prophet denounces and announces.

The third period can be defined as a moment of global fragmentation and a more pluralistic conversation. What distinguishes the third period from the second is again a change in the subject of the theological discourse. Theological voices from the Third World and women start to be brought into the conversation. This started a shift in the prevailing prophetic tone surrounding Evian by overtly admitting that if the responsibility must be shared by all, all have a right to enter the theological conversation. Obviously, this brought along a new sense of democratic participation and representation, as it also signified the eclipse of the hegemony of the professional academicians as well as a fragmentation in the theological conversation. In its 1995 meeting in Windhoek, Namibia, the Executive Council of the LWF received a document entitled "Ten Theses on the Role of Theology in the LWF" prepared by the Program Committee for Theology and Studies. Theses 6 and 7 set the tone for the way theology should be defined and practiced:

> 6. In the history of the LWF as a communion of churches, the awareness of the tension between the gospel that holds us together and the diversity by which we express it grew as creative challenge for both the self-understanding of the LWF as a communion and for its theological practice.

> 7. This challenge offers new opportunities for the exercise of theology in the LWF through which the communion will be promoted if, and only if, these characteristics of theological practice are followed: a) the LWF offers itself as a place for different articula-

tions of diverse experiences; b) as a catalyst for inno-
vation within theologies in different contexts; and c)
as a guarantor of both the diversity and of the necessity of expressing commonalities.[8]

Hong Kong (1997) does not seem to represent any new
breakthrough but a consolidation of some trends in which the
most important seems to be a return to an understanding of
mission dissociated from service, something that had been
strongly argued since Evian. Yet it seems relevant that of the
22 persons that formally addressed the assembly fourteen
were from the Third World while eight came from the North
Atlantic world, though only five women (and only two from
the Third World) were among them.[9]

Broad Strokes

The general movement went beyond prophetism to the
recognition of the voice of the other and particularly those
whose voices have been traditionally muted, rendered unin-
telligible in the official centers of theological dissemination.
The analogy that comes to mind here is the story of the
people of Shem as narrated in Genesis 11. The attempt to
build the tower that would reach heaven, the tower, as it
were, that would raise the great systems of theological knowledge, that would control this knowledge with a single voice,
that would disseminate this knowledge, ended up in its fragmentation. The monophonic movement of dissemination
broke down, opening up a world of multiple voices. The
system can no longer be completed. The people of Shem
seeking dissemination of its procured view from heaven are
desheminized. As a founding myth about human communication, the story of Genesis invites us to recognize multiplicity,
the other voices that disturb the systemic attempts at
univocity. The tale is not a curse but a double warning. On
the one hand, it indicts any grandiose attempt at creating an all-
encompassing system, any single voice of the one who stands
on the top of the tower. On the other hand, it portrays a realistic
view of the difficulties entailed in human communication.

This was the myth retold in different ways in several of the papers here presented. We can read clearly the call to be able to listen and engage in the difficult task of dialoguing with the other who has a different voice, yet belongs to the same people of Shem. We are reminded that that includes the poor, women, the marginalized, the excluded, the foreigner, and yes, even all those who don't even share the basic claim that Jesus is Lord. The challenge of making these voices intelligible and their plight heard requires that the knowledge of the "sage" be put to the service of this task. We are reminded about the need to engage the sciences, ethnology, economy, sociology, philosophy, linguistics, religious studies, anthropology, but also literature, mythology, poetry, music, and art, in order to create intelligibility. But it requires also the task of the prophet in denouncing the systems that have used this knowledge for the controlling powers that create exclusion. As Barbara Rossing reminds us in her Biblical Reflection, even for a prophet, it takes courage to pass the mantle on and walk with the people. It requires also sensitivity and vulnerability to stand before the other and pay attention to the images with which heis or her language is woven. It requires a movement of the Spirit to listen, as strange Galileans were being understood, as the miracle of listening is narrated to us in the story of Pentecost. That the miracle of listening was the founding of the church was a lesson that we were again reminded of here.

Another stroke being drawn in these paper was expressed with several images that spoke about liminality, of being at the edge of the chaos, at the point of crisis, at the limit that defines exclusion, that establishes the rules of difference, a sense of being betwixt and between, even at the point in which language reaches its limits; where poetic and pictorial language is called upon to force open a limit to rational concepturality and seelanguage as a space of possibility. I read language in a call for an eschatological renewal of theology, for images that lift up the eschatological dimension of language. The word apocalyptic was not used. In fact, there was a clear criticism being raised in connection with the millennium ideology with its Armageddonian imagery that saps the energy from the actual and all too familiar Armageddons, in which the oppressed and excluded of the world live. But indeed there was apocalyptic imagery of a different sort that was being used. What is happening I regard to be a basic tectonic shift in theology, a massive shift not clearly visible, but indeed drastic. This shift is represented by a move from an exclusive time and future-oriented eschatology to spatial and geographic imagery.

The eschaton is not only a time in which an end will occur, it is the places in which the end is experienced, in which the limits of one's existence, one's language, one's home, one's land, one's culture, one's resources, one's religion, one's sexual orientation, is met. This is the place of crisis. But instead of lamenting it, instead of whining over it, there is a clear sense of hope that the place designated as the end is also the place of a beginning, that where the last (*eschatoi*) are to be found there also the first (*prothoi*) announce their presence. I think the call is for a radical contextual theology in which context is not simply circumstance (much less pomp) but a qualified place that marks the end of the old and the beginning of a new space. This space is barely more than an edge. It is indeed, however, the edge where the world ends, but also the place where it begins. If there is a hope, this is the message we heard. It is there where we normally have only hopelessness. If there is a salvation it is there where we have seen perdition. In the divide is the divine.

Finally, a third stroke can be recognized. Theology, if it is to bear its name, has to be done at the foot of the cross. Yet, against so many theologies of the cross, the voices we heard, the accents we grew accustomed to, were not praising suffering, were not even speaking about a preferential option for those who suffer. The call was more radical. It was a call to encounter God's own self in that moment, in that limit where the cross is itself a crossing, a crossing toward resurrection. With this the theological task changes. Books and libraries, lectures and documents are not the source of theology, but a means. Indeed valuable means to express it, and valuable to the extent they are able to utter and give language to this experience of the limit. Not the experience of religious epiphanies, of rapture and mystical awakenings, the *tremendum et fascinans*, but the all too-common experience of human suffering and marginalization. At the cross we experience the pedestrian fact that people suffer hunger, are naked, are in prison, are sick, and one might add, the other attributes that are so scandalous exactly because the God we have confessed is to be found in these most trivial experiences of pain.

If theology has to be done in this key as suggested, it will have to be rigorous, informed and even erudite to the point of allowing the disturbing noise of other voices to break into the elaborated discourses of the academia with its empty tombs that, as we were reminded, should not point to themselves but to the living stones that have witnessed the resurrection. On his 80th birthday the Spanish poet León Felipe, reflecting about his life-long exile in Mexico, expressed this courage of reaching the limit with tears in the eyes. And he says something like this:

> When my tears reach it, the function of my eyes will no longer be of crying but of seeing. All the light of the universe, the divine, the poetic, that which we seek, we will see through the window of some shed tears.

If there is a vision, and if that was the pretentious assignment implied in the title of this address, I will not be the one to give it. It is the people, those of other faiths, the women, the displaced in their own land and elsewhere, the poor of the earth, those of other cultures, those of different colors, all those whose voices were represented and articulated by this collection of papers are those who will weave it together. They are painting in the details. The task is only beginning; the trajectory is hereby given. Are we ready to accept the gift?

Epilogue: A Biblical Perspective

Christine Grumm

Luke 7: 36-50

One of the Pharisees asked Jesus to eat with him, and he went into the Pharisee's house and took his place at the table. And a woman in the city who was a sinner, having learned that he was eating in the Pharisee's house, brought an alabaster jar of ointment. She sat at his feet, weeping, and she began to bathe his feet with her tears and to dry them with her hair. Then she continued kissing his feet and anointing them with the ointment.

Now when the Pharisee who had invited him saw it, he said to himself, "If this man were a prophet, he would have known who and what kind of woman this is who is touching him—that she is a sinner."

Jesus spoke up and said to him, "Simon, I have something to say to you."

"Teacher," he replied, "Speak."

"A certain creditor had two debtors; one owed five hundred denarii, and the other fifty. When they could not pay, he canceled the debts for both of them. Now which of them will love him more?"

Simon answered, "I suppose the one for whom he canceled the greater debt."

And Jesus said to him, You have judged rightly."

Then turning toward the woman, he said to Simon, "Do you see this woman? I entered your house; you give me no water for my feet, but she has bathed my feet with her tears and dried them with her hair. You gave me no kiss, but from the time I came in she has not stopped kissing my feet. You did not anoint my head with oil, but she has anointed my feet with ointment. Therefore, I tell you, her sins, which were many, have been forgiven; she has shown great love. But the one to whom little is forgiven loves little."

Then, he said to her, "Your sins are forgiven."

But those who were at the table with him began to say among themselves, "Who is this who even forgives sins?"

And he said to the woman, "Your faith has saved you; go in peace."

This is a story rich with possibilities. One could focus on the cerebral questions of Jesus as prophet—what exactly was being revealed at the time and place of this story, who believed it and who did not, how is one person more sinful than another or are they? Or, one might rather take up the action-side of this story and apply it to how we might envision our lives together as a Lutheran Communion in the twenty-first century. And, since as Lutherans our tendency is to be far more cerebral in our theological interpretations than action-oriented, I think we might take up the challenge of the action-side of this story.

A week ago, I had the pleasure of sitting in an audience of about 500, listening to the powerful and melodic sounds of Sweet Honey and The Rock. A group of five African-American women singers where celebrating the 25th anniversary of their founding. As the show opened, one of the song leaders began to sing, beating out the rhythms to the first phrases of a Gospel song. She suddenly stopped, got up from her chair, walked to the end of the stage, looked into the eyes of a very quiet audience and asked, "Where are you?" Without waiting for an answer, in a very low loud voice she wailed, "What we need here is some disrupting of the still waters." She started clapping, swaying, and inviting the audience to do the same. She kept this up until she had just the right amount of disruption needed to keep the rhythm of her song going and then she started singing again.

Disrupting the still waters—it seems to me, that was indeed the rhythm of the woman seated at Jesus feet in this story. And that is the rhythm of life we need, as a Lutheran Communion, to enter the twenty-first century. While we pride ourselves on our thoughtful and consistent theological under-standings, we are much less thoughtful and consistent when it comes to the rhythm and action-side of our faith. See, I be-lieve our problem, unlike Simon and the other dinner guests, is not so much in believing that Jesus was the prophet, but rather a lack of trust—trust that Jesus will be there when the Gospel rhythm leads us to a place that requires taking a risk and disrupting the order of things. For we are a people of order and consistency, and at times that is in conflict with a Gospel message which calls for the dance of chaos and being about disrupting business as usual.

Changing our rhythm from business as usual to "Disrupt-ing the Still Waters" is how I would like to interlock the Luke story with a look toward our future as a Lutheran commun-ion. Particularly as we think about our place as North Ameri-cans in the global church of the twenty-first century.

To begin, let us go back to the story and look again at the actions of the woman and Jesus. Here is a woman, uninvited to an all-male dinner party, who not only comes into the room, but proceeds to act in a manner unseemly for a woman of that culture. Did the rhythm of those men ever change when she entered that dinner party? It might be compared to group of homeless people walking or slightly staggering up the isle behind the Bishops at Rockefeller Chapel during a great celebration. They have not been invited, yet they feel the presence of Jesus in "our" celebration and want to use this opportunity to be in communion with Jesus. They do the unthinkable, which is to be loud and disruptive in the midst of a well planned, finely tuned ceremony. Their presence changes the entire rhythm of the worship experience. It becomes a rhythm with which many of us would not be very comfortable. What do you think we would do, and what do you think Jesus would do? Would the two be different?

At times, it seems to me, that we work so hard to make the rhythm of the church match our level of comfort and tolerance, as if the very existence of the Kingdom of God is dependent on our maintaining institutional neutrality. We need to remember that the rhythm is not ours, but God's. T.Z. Roo, a Chinese theologian, puts it this way, "The Kingdom of God does not exist because of your effort or mine. It exists because God reigns. Our part is to enter this kingdom and bring our life under God's sovereign will." Stories, like the Luke story before us challenge us to better understand that will of God. Jesus came and disrupted the status quo of the world. Are we not called to do the same?

However, in order to disrupt the status quo, we must understand it and the role we play in keeping that status quo safe and unchanged. If we are to see ourselves as part of a global communion, then we need to see ourselves in light of the global community. How do we stack up in that light? Let us take a look at just one aspect of that human community— the sharing of global resources. According to a new UN Human Development Report, the measuring of the lives of people around the global looks something like this:

1. Americans and Europeans spend $17 billion a year on pet food—$4 billion more than the estimated annual total needed to provide basic health and nutrition for everyone in the world.

2. Americans spend $8 billion a year on cosmetics—$2 billion more than the estimated annual total needed to provide basic education for everyone in the world.

3. At the end of 1997 more than 30 million people were living with H1V. With about 16,000 new infections a day—90 percent in developing countries—it is now estimated that more than 40 million people will be living with HIV in 2000.

How is this picture out of sync with the rhythm of God's vision for the People of God? Bishop Claver of the Philippines answers that question, this way,

At the table of life we share most *disproportionately* indeed. Some go hungry. Others are besottedly full.

The quality of rice we eat is according to the wealth we bring with us to the table. And we eat only with people of our own kind. We do not have enough respect for the community of God. We embarrass the poor outrageously. This is our world. A world of plenty and want, of staggering riches and even more staggering poverty. And into this confused and confusing world comes the stranger seeking to pitch his tent among us.

How much are we willing to disrupt the still waters to change how we sit at the table? How might we act differently as a church—as people of God? Just as Jesus affirmed the woman in her actions—do we do the same for those in our communities that dare to disrupt the still waters, thereby changing the rhythm of the community?

We can preach justice to the world, but our words are hollow if we do not practice it from within. We can preach economic parity, but our words are hollow if we do not understand our institutional role to maintain the status quo. We can preach against violence, but our words are hollow if we do not understand how both our silence and our use of words have contributed to that violence, particularly in the case of people of color, women, gays, and lesbians.

Are we willing to disrupt the very nature of our own institutions to make room for those disenfranchised? To do so will most definitely change the rhythm of who we are and what we do. The rhythm change is often not the most comfortable for us, but remember this is God's Kingdom, not ours. We are dancing to God's rhythm.

Jesus did not play it safe during his ministry here on earth and somehow I think we are called to follow in that same manner. The Division for Global Mission is developing its long-range plan, and one of the most exciting aspects of this plan is the emphasis on the word accompaniment. It is the creation of a new rhythm for our global relationships. It will be new way of being part of the global Lutheran\Christian communion. It calls us to walk with and be part of the lives of Lutheran\Christian communities around the world. It means that we, like Jesus, acknowledge and value the assets that all bring the table. It means we no longer embarrass the poor. It means that we, like Jesus, are willing to pitch our tents in the midst of the community, not outside of it, thereby putting distance between us and them. If we take this way of being in communion seriously, it will be a disruption of the still waters. But, the disruption that will bring new life and energy into our congregations and other expressions of church life.

How willing are we to disrupt the still waters and take the risks that come from a full understanding of the salvation story? Are we as courageous as the woman who, uninvited, entered the room full of men? Are we as strong in our faith, believing that Jesus will accept the gift of ointment or whatever we deem precious to bring to the table? Are we as humble as she to wash Jesus' feet as an act of repentance?

The story does indeed have a tricky rhythm to it, because it requires getting three things going at the same time. For some of us are great at disrupting the still waters, but miss in the humility department, and others of us are humble but forget to act; and yet another set of us act out of our humility but have a difficult time accepting God's grace and forgiveness. The "sinful woman" got it all right. She understood the salvation story in its entirety.

She was disruptive, humble, and accepting of God's grace. Her simple story gives us a focus for the next century. Whose rhythm will we employ to move us forward? The rhythm of the world or the rhythm of the salvation story? If we pick the salvation story, we need to be willing to be in places where we are uninvited, taking action that stirs up the still waters, all the while trusting that the rhythm of God's Kingdom will keep us going.

Contributors

Barbara Rossing. Professor of New Testament, Lutheran School of Theology at Chicago.

Ishmael Noko. General Secretary, Lutheran World Feceration. The Rev. Noko is a member of the Evangelical Lutheran Church in Zimbabwe.

Dorothy Marple. Former Chair of LWF Commission of Mission and Development, former Secretary of the Lutheran Church in America.

William Lesher. Former President, Lutheran School of Theology at Chicago—1978-1997.

Musimbi Kanyoro. General Secretary, World YWCA.

José David Rodríguez. Professor of Systematic Theology and Director of Hispanic Ministry, Lutheran School of Theology at Chicago.

Paul Rajashekar. Professor of Systematic Theology, Lutheran Theological Seminary at Philadelphia.

Mitri Rahab. Director of Dar al-Kalima Academy, Bethlehem

Volker Griefenhagen. Professor of Religious Studies, Luther College and University of Regina, Saskatchewan, Canada.

Molefe Tsele. Executive Director, Ecumenical Service for Socio-Economic Transformation, South Africa.

Karen Bloomquist. Director of Theological Studies of LWF

Monica Melanchthon. Gurukul Lutheran Theological College, Chennai, India.

Wanda Deifelt. Vice Rector, Escola Superior de Teologia, Soa Leopoldo, Brazil.

Vítor Westhelle. Professor of Systematic Theology, Lutheran School of Theology at Chicago.

Christine Grumm. **Director of the Women's Funding Network, San Francisco; former Deputy General Secretary for Planning of LWF; Past Vice President of the Evangelical Lutheran Church in America.**

End Notes

Foreword: A Biblical Reflection

1. Josephus, Against Appion 1.41.

Fifty Years of LWF Mission and Service

1. *From Federation to Communion: The History of Lutheran World Federation,* ed. Jens Holger Schjorring, Prasanna Kumari, and Norman Hjelm (Minneapolis: Fortress Press, 1997).
2. Brakemeier, Gottfried, "Address by the LWF President," in *Official Report of the Ninth Assembly of the Lutheran World Federation,* Hong Kong, July 8-16, 1997, Geneva: Lutheran World Federation Communication Service, 1997, p.10.
3. Solberg, Richard W., *As Between Brothers,* Minneapolis: Augsburg, 1957, p.52.
4. Bachmann, E. Theodore, "The Lutheran World Federation," in *Lutheran Churches in the World: A Handbook,* E. Theodore Bachmann and Marcia Brenne Bachmann eds., Minneapolis: Augsburg, 1989, p.34.
5. *Proceedings of the Lutheran World Federation Assembly, Lund, Sweden, June 30-July 6, 1947,* Philadelphia: United Lutheran Publication House, 1948, p.92.
6. For a review of orphaned missions and related issues, see Scherer, James A., "Faithful to the Fundamental Task: Mission in the LWF," in *From Federation to Communion: The History of the Lutheran World Federation,* op.cit., pp.146-149.
7. *Proceedings of the Lutheran World Federation Assembly, Lund, Sweden, June 30- July 6, 1947,* op.cit., p.7. See also pp.70-77 for an account of the farsighted principles and practices for world mission set forth by the Lund Assembly.
8. Appel, Andre, "The Fifth Assembly 1970," in *Sent Into the World: The Proceedings of the Fifth Assembly Of the Lutheran World Federation, Evian, France, July 14-24, 1970,* LaVern K Grosc, ed., Minneapolis: Augsburg, 1971, p.9.
9. Ibid., pp.66-68, 152-153.
10. Ibid., pp.147-150.
11. Ibid., pp.143-144.
12. For a survey of how mission and evangelism emphases were carried out in the post-Evian period, see James A. Scherer, op.cit., pp.154-175.
13. *LWF Executive Committee Minutes, July-August 1989,* ex. 17, p.10 - These have not been printed.

Lutheran Communion in a Multicultural Identity

1 See for example, most recently Hansen (1998), Melanchton (1998) and Schurg (1998) all in LWF Studies Series, "Communion, Community and Society" (1998)

2 At the assembly in Hong Kong, the history book *From Federation to Communion* was launched. It documents the progress of the discussion that led to the change of understanding and also the activities that bound the LWF together for the last 50 years.

3 Thangaraj, Thomas M., "Globalization, World Religions, and Theological Education," in *Theological Education*, Vol 35, No. 2, Spring 1999, p 144. Professor Thomas Thangaraj of Candler School of Theology, Emory University does not deal with details of those implications but does an excellent job defining how churches can have forward looking visions in mission, while affirming the positive aspects of Globalization as the Elimination of distance.

4 Russell, Letty, *Church in the Round: Feminist Interpretation of the Church* (Louisville: Westminster John Knox Press, 1993), p. 196.

5 Else Marie Wiberg Pedersen, "Ecclesiology and 'koinonia': The folkekirke in Denmark" in LWF Studies: *Communion, Community, Society* (Geneva: Lutheran World Federation, 1998) p. 56.

6.General Secretary of Lutheran World Federation 1984-1994 and currently the bishop of Oslo, in the Church of Norway. It was during his time that most of the discussion on the Communion and the resolution for LWF churches to adopt a new self-understanding as communion took place (in the Eight Assembly in Curitiba, Brazil, 1990.)

7. Staalsett 1987: Manuscript.

8. Mugambi, 1998: 31. African theologians have been saying a similar story through the theology of inculturation.

9. Conference on World Mission and Evangelism/WCC World Missionary Conference, Bangkok, 1973.

10. Dictionary of Feminist Theologies, ed. Letty Russell and and J. Shannon Clarkson (Louisville: Westminster John Knox Press, 1996), p. 26.

Communion and Interfaith Relationships

1 "Religious Pluralism and Lutheran Theology," ed. by J.Paul Rajashekar, *LWF Report*, 23/24, 1988; *Theology in Dialogue*, eds. J. Paul Rajashekar and Satoru Kishii, Geneva: LWF, 1987; "Theological Perspectives on Other Faiths," ed. by Hance Mwakabana, *LWF Documentation*, 41/1997.

2 *Proceedings of the Fourth Assembly of the Lutheran World Federation* (Helsinki, 1963), Berlin: Lutherisches Verlaghaus, 1965, pp. 248-254.

3 *Ibid.*, pp. 261-62

4 *Ibid.*, pp. 352-57; see Appendix III for the final version approved by the Commission on Theology, pp. 476-82.

5 *From Federation to Communion: The History of the Lutheran World Federation.* Eds. Jens Holger Schjorring, et al. (Minneapolis: Fortress Press, 1977). P. 190.

6 *Ibid.*, pp. 189ff.

7 Ulrich Duchrow, *Conflict Over the Ecumenical Movement* (Geneva: World Council of Churches, 1981).

8 *The Identity of the Church and Its Service to the Whole Human Being,* Final Reports (Geneva: LWF, Department of Studies, 1977).

9 See *Christianity and New China*, ed. Arne Sovik (Pasadena: Ecclesia Publications, 1976); *Encounter of the Church with Movements of Social Change* (Geneva: LWF, Department of Studies, 1977).

10 *Christian Witness and Jewish People*, ed. by Arne Sovik (Geneva: LWF, Department of Studies, 1976).

11 One response to this recommendation was a consultation on *Confessing Christ in Cultural Contexts* (Geneva: LWF, Department of Studies, 1981). This discussion was undertaken in the framework of Christ and culture debate and did not focus on issues of other faiths.

12 *In Christ a New Community, Proceedings of the Sixth Assembly of LWF* (Geneva: LWF, 1977), pp. 203-205.

13 *In Christ Hope for the World*, Proceedings of the Seventh Assembly (Geneva: LWF, 1985), p.198.

14 Kenneth Cracknell, *Towards a New Relationship* (London: Epworth Press, 1986), pp. 11-12.

15 For an interpretation of the Nairobi debate, see S.J. Samartha, *Courage for Dialogue* (Geneva: WCC, 1981), pp. 49-62.

16 See the "Preface" in Religious Pluralism and Lutheran Theology," *LWF Report* 23/24, p. 6.

17 Besides the studies noted in footnote 1, other studies included: *Church and the New Religious Movements*, eds. Allan Brockway and J. Paul Rajashekar (Geneva: WCC, 1987); *Christian Muslim Relations in Eastern Africa*, ed. J. Paul Rajashekar (Geneva: LWF, Department of Studies, 1988); *Encounter of Religions in African Cultures* (Geneva: LWF, Department of Theology, 1991); *Islam in Asia*, eds. J. Paul Rajashekar and Henry Wilson (Geneva: LWF and WARC, 1992).

18 See the summary report in "Religious Pluralism and Lutheran Theology, *LWF Report* 23/24, pp. 181-190.

19 Proceedings of the Eighth Assembly, Curitiba 1990, *LWF Report* 28/29, 1990, p. 83.

20 *Ibid.*, p. 84.

21 *Ibid.*, p. 83.

22 *Official Report of the Ninth Assembly, Hong Kong 1997* (Geneva: LWF, 1998), p. 53, emphasis added.

23 *Ibid.*, pp. 107-114.

24 See Michael Root, "Affirming the Communion: Ecclesiological Reflection in the LWF," in *From Federation to Communion*, pp. 216-246.

24 See Article I.

25 *LWF Documentation* 32, 1993

26 "The Church as Communion," *LWF Documentation* 42/1997, pp. 27-29.

27 *Ibid.*, p. 27.

28 *Ibid.*, p. 28

29 *Ibid.*, p,23, emphasis added.

30 J. Paul Rajashekar, "Dialogue with People of Other Faiths and Ecumenical Theology," *The Ecumenical Review*, 39 (October 1987): 455-461.

Communion and the Holy Land and Response

1. Mitri Rahab, *I am a Palestinian Christian* (Minneapolis: Fortress Press, 1995).

2. Norman Habel, *The Land is Mine: Six Biblical Land Ideologies* (1995)

3. These remarks are based on an unpublished lecture given by John Ralston Saul on September 17, 1998 at the University of Regina: "The Layering of Canada: Founding Myths in the Construction of a Complex Civilization" (The 1998 Luther Lecture presented at Luther College).

4. I am especially thinking here of Americans, since the U.S.A. expends a major amount of its foreign aid, especially military, in support of the state of Israel.

Communion within Economic Disparity

1. Memorandum of the EKD. Common Good and Self Interest: Economic activity and Social Responsibility for the Future, 1992.

2. EKD Memo: 12.

3. Memo: 62.

4. Gustavo Gutierrez, *The Truth Shall Make You Free* (Maryknoll, NY: Orbis Books, 1990), p. 7.
5. *Luther's Works* vol. 46 p. 22.
6. *Ibid.* p. 23.
7. *Ibid.* p. 29.
8. *Ibid.* p. 23.
9. Douglas John Hall, *Has the Church a Future?* (Philadelphia: Westminster Press, 1980), p. 80.
10. Douglas John Hall, *Has the Church a Future?* (Philadelphia: Westminster Press, 1980), p. 109.
11. *Ibid.*
13. Gustavo Gutierrez, *The Truth Shall Make You Free* (Maryknoll, NY: Orbis Books, 1990) p. 143.

Communities of Women and the Lutheran Communion

1. Katherine E. Zappone, "'Woman's Special Nature': A Different Horizon for Theological Anthropology," in *The Special Nature of Women?* Anne Carr and Elisabeth Schussler Fiorenza, Eds. Concilium 1991/6 (Philadelphia: Trinity Press International, 1991): 92.
2. Ina Praetorius, " In Search of the Feminine Condition," in The Special Nature of Women?   3.
3. *Ibid.*
4. Anonymous, "From Jaini Bi - With Love," in *Voices of Women: An Asian Anthology*, Alison O'Grady, ed. (Singapore: Asian Christian Women's Conference, 1978), 11.
5. Cf. Jerome Binde, "Challenges for Mankind: Ready for the 21st Century?" in *The Sunday Times*, (September 13, 1998) 36.
6. Lakshmi Daniel, "A Word from DAGA," in DAGA INFO No. 89 (Jan-Feb 1998): 1.
7. Vandana Shiva, *Staying Alive: Women, Ecology and Survival in India* (New Delhi: Kali for Women, 1989).
8. Vandana Shiva in an article on the patenting of life forms through the GATT Agreements for Resurgence, Publication of the Third World Network.
9. I offer this alternate translation from the Hebrew, which uses feminine participles and verbs.
10. Cf. Musumbi Kanyoro, "Communities of Gender and the Communion of the Church," in *Communion, Community, Society*, ed. Wolfgang Grieve (Geneva: LWF, 1998).
11. Musumbi Kanyoro, "Does the LWF Need a Gender Desk? A discussion paper for the LWF," in *The Unfolding Vision: An Evaluative Report on the LWF/DMD Desk for Women in Church and Society 1988-1997*, (Geneva: LWF, 1998) 66.
12. Cf, Musumbi Kanyoro, " Appendix 4: Does the LWF Need a Gender Desk or a Women's Desk?" 59-69.
13. Sandra Harding, "Gendered ways of Knowing and the "Epistemological Crisis" of the West" in *Knowledge, Difference and Power. Essays inspired by Women's Ways of Knowing*. Nancy Goldberg, et.al, Eds. (New York: Basic Books, 1996) 434-37.
14. Cf. Gabriele Dietrich, *Women's movement in India: Conceptual and Religious Reflections*, (Bangalore: Breakthrough Publications, 1988) 129ff.
15. Violet Cucciniello Little, "The Past as Prologue: Women in the LWF," in *The Continuing Journey: Women's Participation in the Lutheran World Federation*, (Geneva: LWF, 1992) 5.

Communion and Reconciliation

1. *The Church as Communion*. LWF Documentation 42. Ed. By Heinrich Holze. Geneva: LWF, 1997, p. 15.
2. Joao Guimaraes Rosa. *Grande sertao veredas: o diabo na rua no meio do redemoinho*. 30. Ed. Rio de Janeiro: Nova Fronteira, 1988. P. 48.
3. Luther's Works, Vol. 35, p.51f.
4. *The Church as Communion*. LWF Documentation 42. Ed. By Heinrich Holze. Geneva: LWF, 1997.
5. *Luther's Works*, Vol. 35, p.67.
6. LWF Report 28/29, p.81.
7. Joao Guimaraes Rosa, *Grande sertao veredas: o diabo na rua no meio do redemoinho*. 30. Ed. Rio de Janeiro: Nova Fronteira, 1988, p.8-9.
8. Martha Ellen Stortz. "Practicing Christians. Prayer as Formation." Ed. By Karen L.Bloomquist and John R. Stumme. *The Promise of Lutheran Ethics*. Minneapolis: Fortress, 1998. P. 56.

A Vision: Culling Some Prophetic Thoughts

1. *Proceedings of the First Assembly of the Lutheran World Federation* (Lund, 1947). Ed. Sylvester C. Michelfelder. (Philadelphia: United Lutheran Publication House, 1948), p. 96.
2. *Proceedings of the Second Assembly of the Lutheran World Federation* (Hanover, 1952). Ed. Carl E. Lund-Quist (Geneva: Lutheran World Federation, 1952), p. 32.
3. *Proceedings of the Third Assembly of the Lutheran World Federation* (Minneapolis, 1957). Ed. Carl E. Lund-Quist (Minneapolis: Augsburg, 1958), p. 102.
4. *Proceedings of the Fourth Assembly of the Lutheran World Federation* (Helsinki, 1963). Ed. Kurt Schmidt-Clausen (Berlin/Hamburg: Lutherisches Verlagshaus, 1965), pp. 442-43.
5. *Sent into the World: The Proceedings of the Fifth Assembly of the Lutheran World Federation* (Evian, 1970). Ed. LaVern K. Grosc (Minneapolis: Augsburg, 1971), p. 32.
6. "Globalization, World Religion, and Theological Education," *Theological Education,* Vol. 35, Number 2, Spring 1999, p. 144.
7. *In Christ-A New Community: The Proceedings of the Sixth Assembly of the Lutheran World Federation* (Dar es Salaam, 1977). Ed. Arne Sovik (Geneva: Lutheran World Federation, 1977), p. 180.
8. Cf. *Between Vision and Reality,* Lutheran World Federation Documentation 47, ed. Wolfgang Greive (Geneva: Lutheran World Federation/DTS, 2001), pp. 497-498.
9. *In Christ-Called to Witness: Official Report of the Ninth Assembly of the Lutheran World Federation* (Geneva: Lutheran World Federation, 1997).